COCOS ISLAND AND
THE TREASURE OF LIMA

COCOS ISLAND AND THE TREASURE OF LIMA

A Desert Island Myth

STEPHEN COOPER

Copyright Stephen Cooper, 2017
The right of Stephen Cooper to be identified as Author of this work has been asserted by him in accordance with the Copyright, Designs and Patents Act 1988.

ISBN: 1544212372
ISBN 13: 9781544212371

CONTENTS

Introduction · ix

Chapter 1   Cocos Island · 1
Chapter 2   The Making of the Myth · · · · · · · · · · · · · · · · · 11
Chapter 3   British Adventurers ·23
Chapter 4   American Adventurers · 42
Chapter 5   The German Experiment · · · · · · · · · · · · · · · · · ·58
Chapter 6   The Foreign Office ·73
Chapter 7   The Boom Years ·83
Chapter 8   The Sceptic · 107
Chapter 9   The Peruvian Revolution · · · · · · · · · · · · · · · · · 124
Chapter 10 The Myth Revived · 142
Chapter 11 The Greening of the Island · · · · · · · · · · · · · · · 159
Chapter 12 Post-Modernism & Pseudo-Science · · · · · · · · · · 176

Appendix Letters Written by Fitzgerald · · · · · · · · · · · · · · · 189
Sources · 195
Illustrations · 199

*And, Lord, this hous in alle tymes
Was ful of shipmen and pilgrimes,
With scrippes bret-ful of lesinges,
[wallets stuffed full of lies]
Entremedled with tydynges.*

Geoffrey Chaucer,
the House of Fame.

*You can fool all the people some of the time,
and some of the people all the time,
but you cannot fool all the people all the time.*

Abraham Lincoln
& Bob Dylan

INTRODUCTION

In *Earl Fitzwilliam's Treasure Island* John Moorhouse and I told the story of how the 7th Earl Fitzwilliam (1872-1943) travelled to Cocos Island in 1904, ostensibly to look for coal and minerals, but in reality to search for buried treasure. In this book I set out to solve the larger mystery regarding Cocos Island. Was the story that the great Treasure of Lima was taken there in 1821 anything more than a legend?

There is a wide, not to say bewildering, variety of myths and legends about Cocos Island, which lies in the Pacific Ocean, opposite Costa Rica and Panama (see Chapter 1); but, since the the late 19th century, the most commonly accepted version of the story (at least in Britain) concerns an event which supposedly happened during the Peruvian Revolution of 1821. So, when a rebel general approached the city of Lima, the Spanish Viceroy entrusted a British merchant sea-captain, one Thompson, who commanded a brig named *Mary Dear*, with a fabulous collection of precious objects and coin, with a view to conveying it to a place of safety; but Thompson turned pirate and took the treasure to faraway Cocos Island, where he buried it. The legend continues that Thompson was unable to recover the loot, but passed his secret on to a Newfoundlander called John Keating, in the 1840s. Keating returned to Cocos with a companion and recovered some part of the treasure; but not all. He returned, whereas the companion did not; and, before he died, he passed his secret on to a shady character called Nicholas, or perhaps Patrick, Fitzgerald, who passed it on to at least two recognisable historical figures: Admiral Palliser and Commodore Curzon-Howe, both of whom were Royal Navy men (see Chapter 2).

In the last quarter of the 19th century, the idea of going to Cocos Island - to see if the Treasure of Lima could be found and recovered - really caught on in Britain. The process was probably assisted by Britain's dominance of the Oceans and her far-flung Empire, but also by the popularity of fictional tales of adventure such as Robert Louis Stevenson's *Treasure Island* (1882). The years 1903-5 in particular saw several expeditions set forth from British shores, some of which arrived in the area before the others had gone, with inevitable disputes as to their right to excavate, especially since there was also a Governor, August Gissler, who was *in situ* at the same time. Gissler was German, but had been appointed by the Costa Rican Government (see Chapter 3).

The Americans were somewhat slower to start, but they also became involved in the hunt. However, though some of them went in pursuit of the Treasure of Lima, others were convinced that there were other pirate hoards to be found on Cocos Island. Then, in the middle of the 20th century, several generations after the supposed events of 1821, the adventurer James Alexander Forbes IV revealed that he was the great-grandson of Captain Thompson's first mate, J. A. Forbes I, who had gone on to find fame and fortune in California. Forbes IV mounted several expeditions (see Chapters 4 and 7).

As for Gissler, he found Cocos Island after hearing a different legend altogether. This certainly involved pirates and buried treasure, but did not include Thompson, his mate or the brig *Mary Dear*. Unfortunately, his 18-year search for the treasure (the longest to date) proved no more successful than all the others (Chapter 5).

All these adventurers set out with high hopes but returned with empty pockets, and by 1914 some historians and newspaper columnists had begun to be sceptical. Yet strangely, the faith which true believers had in the project was restored in 1920, and by the British Government. A Peace Handbook commissioned by the Foreign Office and published by Her Majesty's

Stationery Office appeared to confirm that the Treasure of Lima existed and had indeed been taken to Cocos Island, where it probably still remained (Chapter 6). The consequence was that, in the 1920s and '30s, the number of expeditions multiplied rather than declined. Indeed, there was something of a 'boom' in treasure-hunting, which does not seem to have been substantially affected by the publication in 1935 of a devastating critique of the whole enterprise by Admiral Chambers (Chapters 7 & 8).

Treasure-hunting on Cocos Island revived after the interruption caused by the Second World War (Chapter 10); and even today, despite the 'greening' of the Island, and the prohibition of further excavation (Chapter 11), there are still those who believe, not only that there is treasure to be found on Cocos Island, but that what lies buried there is the Treasure of Lima (Chapter 12).

As the reader will soon discover, I do not share the faith. In particular, I do not think that the traditional legend, or any of its variants, is consistent with the evidence as to what actually happened in Lima in 1821, which has not been examined in any detail before (Chapter 9). My full reasons for doubting the truth of legend are set out in Chapter 12. I would love to be proved wrong.

Chapter 1

COCOS ISLAND

The British have long been interested in desert islands, perhaps because our own Islands are so far from being deserted, even in their least populated parts. From the time of Daniel Defoe's novel *Robinson Crusoe* (1719) to the stage play *The Admirable Crichton* (1902), and the radio programme *Desert Island Discs* (now in its 65th year), we have been fascinated by the problem of how we might survive on such an island, either alone, or with a group of shipwrecked companions.

Generally, the imaginary isle is situated in a warm latitude and resembles the Garden of Eden. This contrasts markedly with the life lived, for example, by the original 'maroons', who were sailors expelled from their community by buccaneers in the age of piracy. Their life was often, in Eric Hobsbawm's phrase, 'no bed of roses'.[1] As for Cocos Island, many who have gone there have found the conditions extremely unpleasant. It rains, nearly all the time. The interior is almost totally overgrown with dense vegetation and there are pests – red ants, rats, cats, and wild pigs, the last three species having escaped from the vessels of previous visitors. Moreover, it is very difficult to land on the Island; and extremely dangerous to swim in the sea, because of the large number of sharks.

---

1 Hobsbawm, *On History* (1997), chapter 15.

However, what brought most to the Island was not a dream, but the promise of riches. Specifically, they hoped to find buried treasure. Cocos Island was more of a modern day *El Dorado* than an Eden or Shangri-La.

LOCATION, GEOLOGY AND CLIMATE

Cocos Island is volcanic in origin, which makes one suspicious of any idea that it might have had workable coal seams, as the 7th Earl Fitzwilliam once claimed. The opening paragraph of H.M.S.O.'s publication of 1920 described it as follows:

> COCOS ISLAND lies in the eastern Pacific Ocean in latitude 5° 35' north, and longitude 87° 2' west. The nearest point on the mainland of Central America is Cape Salsipuedes in the Republic of Costa Rica. Its distance from Panama is about 540 miles. The island is about 4½ miles long and 14 miles in circumference. Its area, including that of a few islets off its coast, is 18 square miles.
>
> The island is mountainous and entirely volcanic, rising to several peaks, of which the highest reaches 2,788 ft. These peaks are probably volcanoes, but the interior is unexplored and almost impenetrable, owing to its steep, rugged, and often precipitous nature, the many rushing streams, and the dense vegetation. There are small areas of comparatively level ground surrounding Chatham and Wafer Bays.
>
> There are many considerable streams, the largest being that which enters Wafer Bay, which is reported to flow from a lake in the interior. Another notable stream enters Chatham Bay, and there is a third on the south coast which has a fall of about 1,000 ft. into a bay behind Meule Islet (see Map which follows).

The Island is in the same Ocean as Robinson Crusoe Island, the second largest of the Juan Fernández Islands, but the two islands are over 2,000 miles apart, since Cocos is opposite Costa Rica and Robinson Crusoe opposite Chile, and they lie on opposite sides of the Equator. A geological survey, published in

COCOS ISLAND AND THE TREASURE OF LIMA

1968 and conducted by Dr Dalrymple of the U.S. Geological Survey and Dr Cox of Stanford University, took lava samples and estimated that the Island had probably been formed in the last million years, and could have formed a bridge for living creatures on their way from the mainland of Central America to the Galapagos Islands, where Charles Darwin conducted much of his early research.[2]

Some of the early explorers were pleased, though also surprised, by what they found. William Dampier, who served on the *Batchelor's Delight* in 1684, pointed out that the Island was named

> by the Spaniards, because there are abundance of Coconut Trees growing on it. They are not only in one or two Places, but grow in great Groves, all round the Island, by the Sea. This is an uninhabited Island, it is 7 or 8 Leagues round, and pretty high in the middle, where it is destitute of Trees, but looks very green and pleasant, with an herb called by the Spaniards *gramadael*. It is low Land by the Seaside. This Island is environed with Rocks, which makes it almost inaccessible: only at the N.E. End there is a small Harbour where Ships may safely enter and ride secure. In this Harbour there is a fine Brook of fresh Water running into the Sea.[3]

The following year, Lionel Wafer found that

> the middle of Cocos Island is a steep hill, surrounded with a plain declining to the sea. This plain is thick set with cocoanut trees; but what contributes greatly to the pleasure of the place is that a great many springs of clear and sweet water, rising to the top of the hill, are there gathered as in a deep large basin or pond, and the water having no channel, it overflows the verge of its basin in several places, and runs trickling down in pleasant streams. In some places of its overflowing, the rocky side of the hill being more perpendicular and hanging

---

2 *The Times*, 27 January 1968.
3 H.M.S.O, Appendix.

over the plain beneath, the water pours down in a cataract, so as to leave a dry space under the spout, and form a kind of arch of water. The freshness which the falling water gives the air in this hot climate makes this a delightful place We did not spare the cocoa-nuts.[4]

In 1893, the French naval officer Lièvre was equally enthusiastic.

> The country on each bank is exuberantly beautiful. This undergrowth, which condemns me to wander so painfully in a chaos of rocks and cascades, is of extraordinarily strong growth, and of a richness of colour that fairly dazzles. Everywhere it is a medley of sparkling verdure, a riot of delicate lace-like fronds and branches. Here, tree ferns, lightly notched, crouch low in the shade of great trees; there, a slim palm uprears her roots to spread her plumes above a thick massif of laurels. From all the branches hang clusters of parasites, orchids, bromeliacias, which garlands of lianas and vines protect with their inextricable maze of tendrils.[5]

In similar vein, the ex-British army office, Hervey de Montmorency, described his first sight of Cocos Island in 1903.

> Cocos Island, with lofty peak, abrupt cliff-like shores, and thick tropical vegetation, was displaying its beauty to our admiring eyes. So thick are the trees that from a small distance they appear like moss upon a stone, while here and there cascades of fresh water shoot off the high ground from amongst the undergrowth right into the sea, falling from a height of over a hundred feet.[6]

However, those who stayed for any length of time generally found that the Island was not at all like Tahiti or Hawaii, or any other of thousands of

---

4 See HMSO, Appendix and Ralph D.Paine.
5 Wilkins, 86
6 Montmorency, 183-4.

South Sea Islands, nor like the eponymous *Treasure Island* of Robert Louis Stevenson's bestseller. Lièvre wrote as follows.

> The ants on Cocos bite men cruelly, when the leaves are touched... The waves dash with rage on the shores of the bay between Meule Island and falling cascades fling their rainbows across the sides of Dampier Head. In this large bay a great waterfall dashes and foams from a neighbouring hill (345 m.), and there is no landing on its shores where landcrabs scuttle along the beaches and sidle out of holes in the banks of the streams.[7]

Writing in 1905, Eustace Cooke-Yarborough (who accompanied Earl Fitzwiliam) tells us that, when the *Véronique* dropped anchor in Chatham Bay, the Earl, Admiral Palliser and Captain Brooke went ahead to see if they could recognise any feature described in the Admiral's map; but, after spending half an hour slipping and sliding around, they were forced to return to the ship's boat, in search of a better landing-place, and somewhere to pitch the tents. With the aid of field-glasses, they could all see that the land rose steeply from the sea on all sides and was almost entirely covered with dense vegetation. Moreover, although there were numerous streams, these became waterfalls at the shoreline. They could see only one small piece of level sand which would be suitable for a campsite. They had four boats: a steam launch, a motor boat, a gig or rowing boat and a small shore boat; but the heavy surf meant that they could only get near the beach in the shore boat, and even then, only to a point where the rollers began to break. Then they had to jump into the water, up to their waists. This they did, but somewhat nervously, because they had seen large numbers of sharks in the water and, as Eustace noted

> Beyond the fact that there were a good number of us splashing about, there was nothing to prevent one of the brutes coming into the 3 or 4 ft. of water that we were compelled to stand in.

---

7 Wilkins, 87-90; H.M.S.O), 24.

In his book *My Greatest Adventure* (1932) Sir Malcolm Campbell described similar experiences suffered in 1926.

> The moment we tackled the opposite slope we found that it was almost vertical. It was like going up the side of a house, and we should never have done it had we not been able to cling on to the creepers and pull our-selves up by them. Finally we got to the top and expected to see the big bare rock we were making for. It was nowhere in sight. That is typical of Cocos. It is a most disheartening island. You sweat and scramble up one hill, expecting to see the object of your search when you reach the top. Instead you are faced with another hill, exactly like the one you have climbed, except that it is a little higher. You get to the top of that one and you find another, higher still.

Later on, after more of the same sort of punishment, Campbell summed up his feelings about the Island.

> These three days were absolute slavery. Never shall I forget the appalling hillsides with the thermometer standing at over 115 degrees in the shade and the heat of the sun beating down like a blast from an oven door. Our hands were blistered and burned with the heat, torn and scarred by scrambling up the rocks. Our finger nails were broken and cracked, our bodies pouring with perspiration and our heads swimming.

LANDMARKS IN THE HISTORY OF THE ISLAND

Campbell also describes how there was a legend 'in the South Seas', which told how a number of Incas once established a colony on Cocos Island; and he even thinks that some of their descendants may still have been hiding there in 1926. He bases this on the fact that his dog was strangely upset in the night, and on his *feeling* that there was someone out there in the darkness, watching him.[8]

---

8 Campbell, 196-7; 228-9.

In fact Inca rule never extended into Central America; and the Incas were not mariners, while the distance from Lima to Cocos Island by sea is almost 1,400 miles. Moreover, when their Empire was overthrown by the Spaniards, the Incas did not take refuge in Central America or overseas, but in the remote fastness of Vilcabamba, in present day Ecuador.

Cocos Island never attracted Spanish settlers either, but it did attract the attention of map-makers, from the earliest times of European exploration. In the 17th century, it became a favourite haunt of pirates and privateers. Its popularity can be accounted for by a combination of factors: its isolated yet accessible position, the availability of abundant fresh water, the abundant supply of coconuts, and the absence of native inhabitants.

Although the Island was uninhabited, it was far from being uninhabitable. When Captain William Betagh R.N. called there at the end of 1720, he recorded that he decided to stay, to allow the sick to convalesce.

> January 18, 1721. Anchor in 13 fathoms, white sand. Here all our people and the Marquis *de Villa Roche* got ashore, where we built a house for the sick men. Here is abundance of good fish round the island, which we take pains to catch, the surf being sometimes very great. Our people find here plenty of coconuts, crabs, boobies, and their eggs, this being their hatching time.[9]

With the decline of buccaneering and smuggling on the Spanish American coasts, the South Sea whaling and sealing enterprises developed an interest in the Island: it was in the interests of the whaling firms that Captain James Colnett R.N. visited the Island in the *Rattler* in 1793. Colnett's description is full and picturesque. He characterizes Cocos as 'Otaheite on a small scale, but without the advantage of its climate, or the hospitality of its natives'. Unlike other navigators, Colnett considered Wafer Bay a better anchorage than Chatham Bay, though only for ships of less than 200 tons. He left a pair of goats ashore, as well as a boar and a sow, which 'multiplied greatly in later years'; and he also planted fruit and vegetable seeds.

---

9 Wilkins, 82.

In 1832, Costa Rica decreed that Cocos Island was part of the the Republic, since it was *terra nullius* (or 'no-man's land'). In 1838, Sir Edward Belcher, in command of H.M.S. *Sulphur,* moored in Chatham Bay, and made a thorough survey: the British Admiralty chart of the Island was based on this; but it is noticeable that Belcher seems never to have heard of the Treasure of Lima, or indeed of any treasure at all being on it, despite the fact that he landed there only seventeen years after Captain Thompson's legendary activities. In 1869 the Costa Ricans formally annexed the Island.

1869 also witnessed a curious incident, which indicated that the Island was capable of supporting at least a small population. The background was that, despite the abolition of the slave trade throughout the British Empire by an Act of 1833, slavers continued to trade in human beings for many years thereafter; and in 1862-3 a number of Peruvian vessels had arrived off Easter Island and kidnapped a large number of islanders, to increase the pool of forced labourers employed in gathering on the Chincha Islands, near Callao.[10] However, to its credit, the Peruvian government was not prepared to tolerate the arrival of this cargo of slaves, and decided to take action. The *Glasgow Herald* for 24 October 1863 and *Dundee Courier* for 21 December 1863 each reported that

> Our readers will remember that the Peruvian government, after the kidnapping of natives from the Kanacca Islands had led to troubles with the French, intends to send back those of the unfortunate creatures that had survived the change of climate and other hardships. Two vessels were chartered to convey back the rest, about 500.

Unfortunately, things did not go smoothly.

> One of these vessels had scarcely embarked her share when the smallpox broke out fearfully on board, and after many had died, the remainder were disembarked again and put on board the other vessel, the barque *Adelante*. Captain Grassau, a Peruvian officer, put to sea with 429 men, with the intention to carry his load of miserable

---
10 H.M.S.O., 42.

> human beings back to their native islands. But on the third day out, the small-pox made its appearance, and caused such sad havoc, that the captain, fearing that all would have died before he should be able to reach his destination, made first for the Galapagos Islands, and seeing there was not fresh water nor victuals enough, went to the Cocos Islands,[11] where he landed those that survived on an uninhabited island

The writer goes on to tell us that the island had

> plenty of water, fruits, and wild hogs. That there was sufficient of those things which make life pleasant, shown by the fact that the steward and one of the sailors ran away in order to share with the Kanaccas their fruits, hogs, and wives.

Between 1879 and 1881 Cocos Island became the H.Q. of the Pacific sperm-whale oil fleet; but it was also used by the Costa Ricans as a short-lived penal colony. Excavations conducted in 2011 revealed the vestiges of a house above Chatham Bay, which may have been used as a *Presidio* by the prison guards, although earlier use of the site as a 'panoramic location during the pirate era' cannot be ruled out.[12] From around this time, the Costa Ricans began to grant concessions to adventurers who wanted to land on the Island, to dig for treasure.

In 1895 the Costa Ricans had a hydrographical survey conducted by Captain R McC. Passmore R.N. and the British Admiralty.[13] More important was the Costa Rican sponsorship, between 1889 and 1908, of the German August Gissler, whose career is dealt with more fully later. During the two decades he spent on the Island, he grew bananas, oranges, limes, vines, pines, potatoes, yams, maize and other fruits and vegetables, as well as coffee; made

---

11 This is a mistake: *the Cocos Islands* are an entirely different island chain, in the Indian Ocean.
12 *Arqueología Histórica en la zona de Bahía Chatham, Isla del Coco: un estudio exploratorio* (Revista Herencia vol. 25 (1 y 2), 87-95, 2012); Knobloch, 170, 218.
13 C. Weston, 166.

cigars from his own tobacco, rope from banana fibre, and tannic acid from the bark of the tulip tree.

In 1934 the Costa Ricans issued a series of stamps, which featured the Island, with a view to deriving some revenue, and proclaiming Costa Rican sovereignty more widely.[14] In September 1940 the Costa Rican government suggested to the U.S.A. that it might take a lease of the Island and use it as a base; but at that time, the Americans thought it entirely unsuitable for that purpose. However, after a U.S. Navy B24 crashed there in 1943, they changed their mind and did use the Island as a base for motor torpedo boats.[15] On May 12, 1970 the Island was incorporated into the Central Canton of the Province of Puntarenas by means of Executive Decree No. 27.

---

14   Vergnes (1978), Chapter 30; *The Times*, 21 February, 1936.
15   *The Times*, 7 September 1940; film, 2012.

Chapter 2

THE MAKING OF THE MYTH

It will be argued here that there is no good evidence that there is buried treasure awaiting discovery on Cocos Island; but there is a powerful myth that this is so, and that the hoard most likely to be discovered is 'the Treasure of Lima,' taken to the Island in 1821. What is the origin of this myth?

To find the answer one has to start with the activities of the Conquistadors, who conquered Mexico and Peru in the early 16th century, in the wake of Columbus's epic voyages of discovery. Unlike the Europeans, the Aztecs and Incas who inhabited these territories did not treat gold as a commodity or currency. Their economies were based on barter; and gold was purely ornamental. The Conquistadors were therefore free to take the gold (and silver) away, or dissipate it, once they had taken control of the two great indigenous empires.

The Spanish conquests were amazingly rapid. In South America, Francisco Pizarro first entered Inca territory in 1526, the Spaniards founded Lima as their capital in 1535, and the last Inca stronghold was captured in 1572. Meanwhile Potosi, founded in 1545, was found to have enormous deposits of silver; and, during the second half of the 16th century, it supplied

60% of all the world's silver.[16] An Italian naturalist described Peru as a whole as 'a beggar sitting on a heap of gold',[17] while an anonymous citizen of the U.S.A. described Lima in 1826 as

> the great emporium of trade for the whole Pacific coast of the continent of America, and the grand depot of the metallic regions of South America, into which they have been pouring their wealth for nearly three centuries.

The silver which the Spaniards brought home brought about a price revolution in Western Europe; and it also stimulated a vast expansion of piracy, since it was far easier for pirates to seize the treasure whilst it was still at sea, than it was for them to compete with the Spaniards on land; but, since pirates, buccaneers and privateers operated on the fringes of the law, or else outside it altogether, they needed to keep their operations secret. Publicity attracted unwelcome attention, though it might be useful in spreading terror. The outlaws tneeded refuges where they could hide their ill-gotten gains.

Cocos Island, remote from the mainland and uninhabited, was a magnet for buccaneers in the Age of Piracy. Accordingly, it would not be surprising if one or more pirate ships, after raiding up and down the Americas, had called in there to bury their loot; and, likewise, it would not be surprising (given the nature and perils of piracy), if one or more had failed to come back; but this does not prove the existence of any particular hoard of treasure. It merely explains why the myth arose, and why it has proved so enduring.

THOMPSON

There were three legendary figures who were central to the main myth current in Britain and the British Empire in the 19th century: Thompson, Keating and Fitzgerald. According to this the Treasure of Lima consisted of a vast reserve of gold and silver which the Spaniards had accumulated in their Peruvian

---

16   Williamson, chapter 1.
17   Hobsbawm, *Age of Capital*.

capital, but were unable to bring home to Spain because of the wars of independence in Central and South America. In 1821, when the army of the Liberator José de San Martín was approaching Lima, the Spanish Viceroy is supposed to have entrusted the imperial treasure to a British trader, Captain William Thompson, so that he could convey it to a place of safety in his ship the *Mary Dear* (or *Mary Deer*, or *Mary Dier*). Instead of doing that, Thompson and his crew killed the Viceroy's men and sailed to Cocos Island, where they buried the loot. Shortly afterwards, they were arrested by a Spanish warship and the whole crew (except Thompson and his first mate) were executed for piracy. In exchange for their lives, the two survivors promised to reveal where the treasure was hidden; but, once back on the Island, they ran off into the jungle, from which they eventually escaped, without the treasure.

As he lay dying, in Newfoundland twenty or more years later, Thompson passed his secret to John Keating. This is H.T.Wilkins's version (published in 1932) of how this happened:

> A mysterious seaman supposedly lay dying in the home of a Newfoundland fisherman with whom he had formed a friendship. He signed to the fisherman to bend down, when he handed to him a chart full of directions about a treasure buried in a desert island in mid-ocean…
>
> Thompson then tells how his ship was captured by a Peruvian man-o'-war, and his men shot. He and two of the crew were spared on promising to reveal the location of the cache. They led the warship on a fool's chase to the Galapagos Islands, and on the way out, in the Bay of Dulce, he and another pirate escaped at night and swam to a whaler. "We said nothing about the treasure, and some years later, went home to Nova Scotia."[18]…
>
> Once there," said the chart, "follow the coast line of the bay till you find a creek, where, at high-water mark, you go up the bed of a stream which flows inland. Now, you step out seventy paces, west by south, and against the skyline you will see the gap in the hills. From

---

18 We note that in this version of the story, Thompson is Canadian, rather than Scots.

any other point, the gap is invisible. Turn north, and walk to a stream. You will now see a rock with a smooth face, rising sheer like a cliff. At the height of a man's shoulder above the ground, you will see a hole large enough for you to insert your thumb. Thrust in an iron bar, twist it round in the cavity, and behind you will find a door which opens on the treasure."...

Keating supposedly made no less than three voyages to Cocos Island. Here is Wilkins's narrative of these.

> [First voyage] He told a Captain Boag, or Bogue, who, in his turn, induced two Liverpool men (Smith and Irwin) to charter a brig, the *Edgcombe,* and, with Captain Bogue as skipper,[19] and Keating and one Gault, they sailed for Cocos Island, which they reached in June 1841. Two deserters from an American brig were on the island when Bogue and Keating landed, but whether any treasure was found by the *Edgcombe* is not clear. It is probable that the cave was visited; since Keating, on his return to Newfoundland, gave orders to Kearney, a local man, to build a clipper schooner, *Red Gauntlet* of 120 tons, of 120 tons.
>
> [Second voyage] Bogue again joined him for a second voyage, some time in the early 1840s. They found the treasure cave, and secretly carried to the ship, in canvas pockets sewn inside their clothes, some of the gold. Another version is that, on the return trip, Bogue, his pockets loaded with heavy loot, fell into a hole in the raging surf, when the subsequent proceedings interested him no more; but there were folk who roundly said that Keating had hit Bogue on the head while he was bending down in the treasure cave, and had pushed the heavy door to and left comrade Bogue to die inside....
>
> [Third voyage] Keating made a third trip to Cocos Island, in 1846, and brought off altogether about $110,000. Bogue's son, says one account, found that his father's sea-chest had been rifled and only

---

19 According to H&W, the Captain was called Gould or Gault: H&W, 40.

a small button-bag, containing twenty-seven gems, left; but whether Captain Bogue's sea-chest was picked up in the sea, afloat off Cape Horn, and mailed to St. John's, N.F., by the skipper of the *Flying Dutchman,* doth not appear in this variant.

Twenty years later Keating met Fitzgerald.[20] Fitzgerald had retired from the sea and made no further voyages himself; but he passed the secret on in turn, to the historical figure Henry Palliser (1839–1907), a Royal Navy officer who, following promotion to Captain in 1878, was appointed Commander-in-Chief of the Pacific Station in 1896.

Montmorency gives us a very full account of the part played in these proceedings by Fitzgerald. As we have said, the latter was not an explorer; but he was a letter writer, perhaps a prolific one, and it is certain that he wrote three letters in the 1890s. The first of these was to Sir Assheton Gore Curzon-Howe (1850-1911) and was reproduced by Sir Malcolm Campbell in his book. It was signed by <u>Nicholas</u> Fitzgerald and dated 10 September 1894. It stated that the writer wanted a twentieth part of the gross value of what was 'in the cave', if and when the treasure should be found.[21]

The second letter was written to Palliser, and was reproduced in its entirety by Hancock and Weston. It was signed by <u>Patrick</u> Fitzgerald and, according to Gissler, was received in Lima around 1896. This letter has been thought by some to be a version of the 'Spanish prisoner' confidence trick, where the writer told his victim that he was a wealthy person of high estate who had been imprisoned in Spain. In this case Fitzgerald told Palliser that he had revealed his secret to officers of the Bank of Peru; but had then been kidnapped by persons unknown, who would not release him unless he told them where the treasure was hidden. However, the letter made no demand for money. It merely asked for assistance, appealing to Palliser as a fellow Irishman and British subject, and making it clear that he had already asked the British consul for help, without success.[22]

---

20   Montmorency, Chapter IV.
21   Campbell, 223, 260, 87-89. The letter itself is at pp 91-96; see also Appendix below.
22   Hancock & Weston, 45 (maps); 308-9 (letter).

The third letter, which was again written to Palliser, was reproduced by Montmorency and written by <u>Nicholas</u> Fitzgerald, on 23 May 1898. After describing the treasure cave on Cocos Island in some detail, it gave details of how to find it. This letter is not written in terms which suggest a confidence trick.

But what should we make of the fact that Fitzgerald used two Christian names? Were the two Fitzgeralds even the same person? Hancock and Weston thought they undoubtedly were; and they may be right. In addition, the discrepancy could be accounted for by Montmorency's practice of disguising the true names of his characters. If he was capable of changing Palliser's surname to Shrapnel, he might not have balked at changing Fitzgerald's Christian name, though that would not have been much of a disguise. Perhaps he just made a mistake.[23]

Whilst there is not enough in these letters to indict Fitzgerald for fraud, there is enough to make the reader suspect that he was probably a fantasist.

MRS BRENNAN AND CAPTAIN HACKETT

The myth was subject to variations, and there is one tradition which omits Fitzgerald altogether. According to this, Keating left some papers to his second wife when he died. She re-married and became Mrs Brennan, but formed a partnership with an associate of her late husband's, Captain Hackett. They sailed for Cocos Island on board the *Aurora* in 1894. This was reported in the *Shields Daily Gazette* on 8 September 1897.

SEARCH FOR BURIED TREASURE

A remarkable story of a search for treasure has just come from Victoria, British Columbia. The scene of the romantic story is Cocos Island… The vessel was the *Aurora*, commanded by Captain F. Hackett. She had a crew of eight hands, but the chief personage on board was Mrs Brennan. She was in possession of an old Spanish

---

23 Montmorency, 76-9.

chart of the island where the millions of treasure are said to have been buried.

The legend of this treasure-island goes back to war of emancipation, when the south and Central American Colonies fought against Spain. Then it was that the refugees are said to have carried their riches of gold and silver and buried them at Cocos Island, going four hundred miles over the Pacific Ocean to this place of safety. As years went by and the story of the treasure was retold, expedition after expedition went to seek for it.

When the crew of the *Aurora* landed they found a man named Charles Hartford on the island. He had been there since last September. The *Aurora* returned to Victoria in August, after an absence of six months, the venture being a complete failure. Hartford professed to know where treasure to the amount of 50,000,000 dollars was buried on the island, but as the crew of the *Aurora* would not agree to terms, Hartford refused to divulge the hiding-place.

Now this is interesting because a connection is made here between Keating, or at least his widow, and the Spanish American wars of independence. However, there is no mention of Lima or even Peru, and certainly no mention of Thompson, who is supposed (by those who hold to the main tradition) to have been Keating's informant.

Montmorency's account of the voyage of the *Aurora* added further details.[24]

Hackett would not listen to the old woman, and, when she protested that the men were not working in the right spot, retorted: "Shut up, you old fool, you know nothing!" The *Aurora* expedition suffered great hardships, as the vessel was very small and took forty-three days to reach the island from Vancouver; she was manned by six ex-captains of vessels, all bent on treasure-seeking and, as may

---

24 Wilkins, 97; Montmorency, 70-3. There is also an account of this voyage in C. Weston, 168-9, taken from the Costa Rican newspaper *Diario de Costa Rica*, 21 November 1897.

be imagined, harmony seldom reigned. They were a rough lot, and when they found nothing, in a fury of disappointment they stripped the old woman and searched her clothes, and broke open her boxes, convinced that she possessed some information which she was holding back. Mrs. Brennan, who was bent double with age, contrived to climb to the top of the highground above Wafer Bay, where she stood contemplating the outlook. "This is not the place, boys," she kept repeating, "it ought to be a bay with a small beach shaped like a crescent, with black rocks on either side, where you are hid from the open water."

Before leaving Mrs Brennan, we may note that the man called Harford will re-appear in the accounts of Admiral Palliser's first visit to the Island. We also learn from Robert Nesmith's book that Hackett and a Captain A.B.Whidden embarked on a second voyage to Cocos Island in 1901, and that this was financed by a Canadian concern in British Columbia, The Pacific Exploration and Development Co. Ltd. On this occasion the adventurers used certain instruments claimed to be more or less scientific, namely a 'silver finder' and a 'gold finder', said to be capable of detecting precious metal in small quantities at a distance of 200 yards, and in large quantities at a distance of some miles.[25]

THE ROLE OF FICTION AND ORAL TRADITION

As we have seen, there were material circumstances which helped to turn Cocos Island into a home for buccaneers. Dr Ina Knobloch also thinks that the California Gold Rush of 1848 brought large number of restless men to the West Coast of the U.S.A., some of whom went on to seek wealth and adventure elsewhere. Moreover, she points out that, although there were hundreds of expeditions to Cocos Island between 1850 and 1978, many must have been unofficial, in the sense that no permission of any kind was sought from Costa

---

25 Nesmith, 229.

Rica. Moreover, privateering was discouraged by an international convention signed in 1856; but it continued to be encouraged by the dubious status of Cocos Island in international law.

By the time Keating died in 1882, the world had changed a great deal from the one Thompson had known in 1821. Capitalism, and the industrial revolution, had transformed it. The U.S.A. now had its tycoons and its 'robber barons', while Great Britain had acquired a large new middle class, and even the British aristocracy had acquired new sources of wealth and power. Sailing ships were being replaced by steamers. With the laying of transoceanic cables, electric telegraphy replaced semaphore. Primary education had become compulsory, literacy had increased exponentially and the number of newspapers and magazines had exploded.

Two works of fiction gave a great boost to treasure-hunting. The first was J. Jebb's *The Lost Secret of the Cocos Group*, published in *Blackwood's Magazine* in January 1873. This short story was about Cocos Island (not the Cocos (Keeling) Islands, as the title might suggest); and it purported to be based on fact, though the proper names had been changed; but there is no mention in it of Thompson, nor his mate, nor of the *Mary Dear*, nor of Callao and the events of the Peruvian Revolution. Instead, Jebb tells us about a group of characters gathered around a campfire somewhere near the Chicago Lakes. One of them with pretensions to a medical qualification tells a story to the others late at night.

Years before, he had met an old man who died while in his care, leaving a sea-chest, in which there was a ship's log, and inside it, the clue to finding a hoard of treasure buried on Cocos Island. This is described in some detail, though its provenance is not.

> A pile of Mexican dollars, dozens of bars of pure gold, case after case of precious stones; yes! and gold crucifixes and candlesticks and suchlike; piles of them, for there was more the loot of more than one Spanish town there.

Later on the narrator tells us that

The west coast cities, from San Francisco to Lima, had been flooded with old Spanish coin.

This is the nearest we get to any 'Treasure of Lima'. However, the narrator tells his audience that he made no less than three trips to Cocos Island. On the third occasion, he managed to make a landing; and then, while using the clue left by his erstwhile patient, he contracted jungle-fever and lost consciousness. Three weeks later he awoke in a hospital in Panama, to be told that his companions had never found anything. Some of them determined to return, so convinced were they of the treasure's existence; but our narrator was thoroughly frightened and vowed never to go back. In any event, those around the campfire have all fallen asleep, by the time the narrator finishes telling them his story.

The Lost Secret of the Cocos Group provides no evidence for the existence of the Treausure of Lima; but it does show that there was a legend concerning Cocos Island in the early 1870s, some considerable time before any of the better known and allegedly factual accounts of treasure-seeking came to be written. It may also have served to fire the imagination of those members of the British upper classes who read *Blackwood's Magazine* and had the time and the means to indulge themselves in expensive foreign travel. (One imagines that *Blackwood's Magazine* may have circulated widely in gentlemen's clubs in London and the provinces).

By comparison, the second work of fiction which appeared at this time was in a league of its own. This was Robert Louis Stevenson's *Treasure Island*, which soon became a worldwide 'bestseller'. The novel was originally serialized in the children's magazine *Young Folks* between 1881 and 1882 and first published as a book in November 1883. It rapidly became famous for its references to pirates, treasure-maps, tropical islands, the Black Spot, and a one-legged seaman with a parrot on his shoulder; but it needs to be said that there is no explicit reference in Stevenson's work to Cocos Island, nor for that matter to Thompson, the *Mary Dear*, or the Treasure of Lima.

Stevenson may well have inspired by stories about Cocos Island, particularly those circulating in California, but the only thing which his novel has in common with the traditional myth we are concerned with, is piracy and the usefulness of desert islands as hiding places for hoards of gold and silver. Some writers (see for example Knobloch, below) have pointed to similarities in topography between Treasure Island and Cocos; but parallels have also been drawn with many other islands, in all parts of the world, including Fidra in Scotland.

Stevenson's work contained a moral. At the end of the book, Jim Hawkins reflects

> Oxen and wain-ropes would not bring me back again to that accursed island; and the worst dreams that ever I have are when I hear the surf booming about the coasts, or start upright in bed, with the sharp voice of Captain Flint still ringing in my ears: 'Pieces of eight! Pieces of eight!'

The irony is that in Stevenson's fiction, the hero did not go to Treasure Island voluntarily, and he returned with no desire to go back, ever again; but in the real world, many men and a few women have travelled to Cocos Island of their own free will, in search of adventure as well as treasure; and, although they have always returned empty-handed, they have usually yearned to go back.

There were other works of the imagination which stimulated an interest in travel and exploration at this time. 1873 saw the publication of Jules Vernes's *Around the World in Eighty Days.* The ambitions of would-be adventurers in Victorian and Edwardian Britain were also fed by the novels of Captain Marriott (1792-1848), H. Rider Haggard (1856-1925) and G.A.Henty (1832-1902), and we should also mention J.M.Barrie, whose stage play *Peter Pan* was premiered in London at Christmas 1904 and whose pirates have thrilled small children ever since.

Oral tradition has also played an important role in propagating the myth, especially amongst sailors and seafolk, many of whom were probably illiterate. So, for every seaman who read the stories of Jebb and Stevenson, there were probably many more who listened to yarns, and then repeated what they heard. Moreover, there was a period of some 50 years between Thompson's supposed raid on Callao in 1821 and 1873, which was roughly when serious efforts began to be made to recover the Cocos Island treasure.[26] More than enough time, one would have thought for the story to be corrupted in the telling and re-telling. To anticipate the conclusion which is more fully developed below, it is likely that the tales which were told and re-told by Thompson, and by Keating and Fitzgerald about Thompson, were nothing more than tall stories, not dissimilar to those which had featured in Coleridge's *Rime of the Ancient Mariner* (1798).

---

26 H.M.S.O., 14.

Chapter 3

BRITISH ADVENTURERS

By virtue of her victories over Napoleon, and her possession of the only 'Blue Water' Navy, the United Kingdom became a world power, at the same time as she was becoming 'the workshop of the world'. The world was transformed, by the application of science to industry, and the advent of railways, steamships and telegraphy.[27] The Royal Navy and the British merchant navy were now powered by coal, rather than the wind. Transoceanic cables girdled the earth and coaling stations were set up all around it. The British were in the forefront of exploration, especially on the high seas, and there are signs of interest in Cocos Island, from an early date.

ADMIRAL PIM
Admiral Bedford Clapperton Trevelyan Pim, R.N., M.P., F.R.G.S (1826–1886) was a Royal Navy officer, Arctic explorer, barrister, and author. He tells us about a voyage to Cocos Island in 1849, and we should note that this precedes the 'start date' for treasure-hunting given by Foreign Office historians in 1920, by some 25 years.

---

27 Hobsbawm, *The Age of Capital, 1848-1875* (kindle books).

LUCKLESS TREASURE SEEKERS

As you cannot be many days in the East before you find yourself talking about magicians, so you cannot be many days at Panama, before you at all events catch yourself listening to stories of treasure-trove.

How many expeditions have there not been from Panama and elsewhere to the Cocos Island for the purpose of recovering the treasure buried there by pirates? I remember very well the men who, more than twenty years ago, made the first expedition thither. The prime mover of it was an English carpenter, whose ambition in life, as he often assured me when picking up my natural history specimens, was to become a fellow'of the Royal Society, which was identical in his mind with life at Court; and this ambition, he thought, might be gratified by spending a sufficiently large sum of money on science.

Once, but only once, the object had been almost within his grasp. He had been kind to an old countryman of his, and when the latter was about to die, he confided to him that he had been a pirate, that a large treasure was buried on the Cocos Island, a few hundred miles from Panama, and that on the map which he handed to him the exact spot was indicated. The old man was about to give further particulars, when the carpenter, intoxicated with joy at the prospect of his sudden good fortune, rushed into the open air, capering about like a madman. When reason somewhat returned, he hastened back to the bedside, but the, old pirate had gone to his account, and the details of his revelation were lost for ever.

Nevertheless the carpenter had no difficulty in persuading a Scotch watch-maker, a physician of the same nationality, and a couple of natives to accompany him to the Cocos Island. They collected as many provisions as they could, put them on board a large flat-bottomed canoe, and started. But they soon became aware that such a canoe could never make as long a sea voyage; and, taking a leaf cut of the book of the pirates whose ill-gotten gains they were about to search for, they put themselves alongside a schooner belonging to the New Granadian Government, and so frightened the men in charge that they willingly exchanged the schooner for the canoe.

After many hardships and a lengthened passage, resulting from violent tropical squalls, long calms, and the almost total absence of nautical instruments, they reached the island, and found it uninhabited and densely covered with vegetation. The map had been drawn on so small a scale that it indicated little more than the side of the island on which the treasure was said to be buried. The members of the expedition, nothing daunted, resolutely set to work for several months, digging and blasting, but without finding a trace even of anything.

Now, if Admiral Pim's story contains even a grain of truth, it makes a nonsense of the conventional 'genealogy' current in late 19th century Britain – the idea that Thompson passed his secret to Keating in the 1840s, that Keating passed it to Fitzgerald a generation later, and that the latter then passed it to Palliser and others in the 1890s. One might explain the discrepancy by pointing out that this conventional wisdom relates only to the Treasure of Lima, supposedly taken by Thompson from the port of Callao in 1821, and that the secret imparted by Pim's anonymous pirate to his anonymous English carpenter related to a different hoard altogether. However, we may also wonder whether the encounter between Pim's two anonymities is actually a garbled version of Thompson's meeting with Keating.

But Pim is telling us more than this. His narrative makes it clear that there was already an active treasure-hunt, centred on Cocos Island, before 1850. If so, that may suggest that the origin of all these stories lies in myth rather than history. It is particularly interesting that the note of scepticism sounded in Pim's account was to be echoed about a hundred years later, in an article written by Admiral Chambers. Both writers had long experience of the sea and sailors, and the nature of the tales they told each other, during the long nights at sea or in the tavern.

ADMIRAL PALLISER

Admiral Henry St. Leger Bury Palliser, R.N. (1839–1907) was promoted Captain in 1878 and Rear-Admiral in 1893. He retired in 1899 but was advanced to the rank of Vice-Admiral, and then Admiral, in 1904. According to Montmorency, 'stories [about Cocos Island] reached [Palliser's] ears from all quarters of the globe', including Peru, San Francisco, Samoa and Buenos Aires; and these stories were confirmed 'in every port of the Pacific coast'.[28] It is important to say, however, that Montmorency did not refer to Palliser by name – he called him Captain Shrapnel, just as he referred to Palliser's vessel HMS *Impérieuse* as HMS *Haughty*. This was presumably because Palliser was still alive when Montmorency was writing, and indeed was a V.I.P. It would not have been sensible to refer to such a man by his real name, given that some of the events related, such as Palliser's behavior on Cocos Island, were reprehensible; but, in this case, the use of pseudonyms has been the source of a good deal of confusion.

Montmorency tells us that in 1882 Palliser acquired a map of the Island, purporting to show the exact location of the hoard, though historians also tell us that 'if all [the] documents, charts and maps were laid side by side, they would blanket the island.' Palliser probably acquired the map from Fitzgerald, from whom he also received at least two letters. He certainly seems to have 'bought into' the central British legend regarding the Treasure of Lima, and set out to look for it even before he had retired from the Royal Navy.

The following story appeared in the *St James's Gazette* and the *Edinburgh Evening News* on 4 November 1897:

A TALE OF BURIED TREASURE

A sensational story is published by a New York paper this morning to the effect that her Majesty's cruiser *Impérieuse*, which has just arrived at Victoria, British Columbia, has returned from Cocos Island, whither she went in search of buried treasure. The officers are reported to have stated that the story of a treasure of thirty million dollars

---

28 Montmorency, 82, 85, 88.

being buried in the island is not a myth. A guard of marines has been left on the island, and a smaller vessel than the *Impérieuse* will proceed there shortly. It is reported that the *Impérieuse* has on board a large portion of the buried treasure, consisting of jewellery and gold to the value of about fifteen million dollars.

The next report was more sceptical. *Reynolds's Newspaper* for 7 November 1897 carried the story that:

There is no truth in the reported discovery of a vast treasure on Cocos Island. A party from the vessel searched the island, but failed to discover the treasure, the existence of which is highly doubtful.

Nevertheless, the original story re-surfaced in the *Edinburgh Evening News* for 13 November 1897.

THE TREASURE ISLAND STORY
SIX MILLIONS AWAITING AN OWNER

An engineer on board the *Impérieuse* has sent a letter to his father in Exeter respecting the stories of treasure on Cocos Island, from which seems that there is more truth in the rumours than recently appeared probable.

This island (says the engineer) was a great resort for buccaneers, and during the war between Mexico and Spain, when the Mexicans threw off the Spanish rule, they sent a good part of their treasure in a ship, which was captured by pirates and the treasure buried at Cocos Island. The pirates were at last all killed off but one, who left a chart to some relation of his showing where the treasure was hidden. A man called Harford, descendant of this pirate, has now the chart, and has been hunting for the gold on the island for some time, and at last found the place, but as he had no ship to take it away, and there are four or five other people on the island all hunting for this treasure, he came up to Victoria (British Columbia) to try and get up an expedition, which he couldn't manage. He was introduced to the Admiral,[29] who offered to go down there after the Guatemala revolution was over, and so brought this man down with us from Esquimalt.[30]

We left San José on the 11th and reached Cocos Island on the 14th. We landed a party and proceeded to dig, but though they found the landmarks, the water from a waterfall nearly filled up the hole during night, and it would have been impossible to dig the treasure out in less than month As the Admiral could only wait a couple of days, they had to leave it; but before going they blew down a good part of the cliff with gun-cotton over the hole, so it will take the people on the island about three months to dig it up. Harford intends go back. The gold bars alone are said to be worth 30,000,000 dollars or about £6,000,000, and there are diamonds and other treasures also hidden in different parts of the island.[31]

Now this is an intriguing story, albeit a garbled one. The Treasure of Lima is not mentioned by name, but we are told about a treasure whose security was put in danger by revolution in Latin America, albeit that this revolution supposedly takes place in Mexico, rather than Peru. Moreover, we are told of a pirate who seized the treasure and whose crew suffered the ultimate penalty for his crimes. Lastly, there is a link between the original events and Palliser, in the form of the man Harford, supposedly a descendant of the pirate. Keating is not mentioned.

What are the facts concerning Palliser's first encounter with Cocos Island? According to Hancock and Weston (1960), he first visited the Island in 1897, when he was on the Royal Navy's Pacific Station. While on board *H.M.S. Impérieuse* he made a landing on the Island while its Governor, Herr August Gissler, was temporarily away. Without obtaining permission from the Costa Ricans, he sent several platoons of marines ashore with shovels, picks and

---

29 Palliser.
30 In Canada.
31 The same story appears in the *Northern Whig*, 15 November 1897; and in the *Man of Ross and General Advertiser*, 27 November 1897.

large quantities of dynamite. Ignoring the protests of Frau Gissler, they excavated, blasted large holes in several places, and vandalised the Island for several days, but found nothing. Great Britain may once have been famous for 'gunboat diplomacy' but, with hindsight, this seems more like piracy and Palliser was severely reprimanded by his superiors, though he was also promoted soon afterwards.[32]

Can we believe this? It is possible that Weston got his information from Gissler, who was told about the incident by his wife, and she may have been so frightened by the arrival of the bluejackets that she embellished the story somewhat. However, the source may have been Montmorency, who tells a very similar tale, except that he says that Palliser acted on the suggestion of an anonymous American, who was present in the ward-room on board his ship (doubtless, after some alcohol had been imbibed).[33]

Whatever the exact truth of it, it is extraordinary that Palliser should have been able to indulge his taste for treasure-hunting while he was serving as an officer on a warship in Her Majesty's Royal Navy, when he was supposed to be patrolling and supervising target-practice for his gunners. However, he did not have long to wait before he could indulge his passion quite legitimately. In 1902, only five years after landing his marines on Cocos Island, Palliser retired, and then wrote to the Chairman of the Pacific Exploration Company, offering to reveal where the treasure was, in return for a quarter of the amount to be recovered, and one twentieth for his agent.[34]

A new expedition was mounted; and Palliser gained a place on it, on the strength of his experience, though he does seem to have exaggerated this, if a report in the *Northamptonshire Evening Telegraph* for 29 March 1902 can be believed.

---

32 Hancock & Weston, 122. I could not find any confirmation of these events in Palliser's Journals for 1896-99, though there are around a dozen in TNA ADM 50/359 but there again, one would not expect him to have recorded this kind of event in any official log or journal.
33 Montmorency, 27-9.
34 *Dundee Evening Post*, 5 April 1902.

THE TREASURE-HUNTING EXPEDITION

A correspondent writing from Victoria, British Columbia, gives details of a novel treasure-hunting expedition. He says that there are quantities of buried treasure on Cocos Island, off the coast of Costa Rica... The evidence on the point is quite convincing, and altogether different from that on which innumerable other treasure stories are based.

Admiral Palliser, of the British Navy, admits that he has found the treasure and left marks for identifying it. During the last century several persons removed small quantities of the treasure. The Pacific Exploration and Development Company has been formed in British Columbia for the purpose of searching for this buried wealth. The company expects to recover at least £6,000,000. The barkentine *Blakely* already started out on its search, and by this time her crew may be digging up the gold and jewels. The island lies in the Pacific 550 miles west of the Costa Rica coast.

Admiral Palliser was recently in command of the Pacific Squadron. It is well known that he conducted a search on Cocos Island, where he went with the cruiser *Impériense*. The task of finding a well-buried treasure on an island after many years must be a very difficult one. If Admiral Palliser knows where it is, his assistance may be invaluable. We may perhaps judge the care with which pirates buried their treasure from Poe's "Gold Bug"[35] and Stevenson's "Treasure Island."

The first treasure was deposited at Cocos Island about the year 1821 by a British ship which had turned pirate. History gathered from official sources records the capture, trial amd execution of the leaders. The second and greatest treasure was deposited on Cocos Island by the barquetine *Mary Dea* [sic] bound from Bristol for Valparaiso, in about the year 1835 [sic]. This ship is said to have deposited eleven boatloads of treasure on Cocos Island.

---

35 A short story written by Edgar Allen Poe and published in 1843.

> Admiral Palliser sought the treasure with H.M.S. *Impérieuse* and H.M.S. *Amphion*. ...He found the treasure, and not being able carry a great quantity away he blasted a great deal of neighbouring rock with dynmite, and thus hid the spot where had been working.

This narrative is riddled with errors and inconsistencies. Indeed, it is a salutary reminder of the old maxim that one should not believe everything one reads in the newspapers. However, it did receive a strong counterblast, from an article in the *Dundee Evening Post*.

> The story of a member of the Metropolitan Fire Brigade, who was a seaman on HMS *Impérieuse*, and one of Admiral Palliser's working party at Cocos Island, was a little different. He told a reporter that Admiral Palliser never found the treasure. He found a stone slab, and then the water rushed in and washed the diggers out. Admiral Palliser blew up the ground with dynamite, not because he had found so much treasure that he couldn't carry it away, but in pure vexation because he couldn't find the treasure.

MONTMORENCY
The story of Hervey de Montmorency's voyage to Cocos Island in 1903 is told in his book, *On the Track of A Treasure, The Story of an Adventurous Expedition to the Pacific Island of Cocos in Search of Treasure of Untold Value Hidden by Pirates* (1904)

Montmorency was a Major in the British Royal Artillery, who resigned his commission to pursue an inheritance claim through the Irish Chancery Court, following the death of his grandfather.[36] During the 1890s, he turned his horsemanship into a source of income, having some success with steeplechasers in England and France, and even competing in several Grand Nationals at Aintree. In 1899 he took part in the famous relief of Mafeking. His diary of *The Boer War* (1902) is held in the National Archives at Kew.

---

36 See Montmorency's *Sword and Stirrup, Memoirs of an Aventurous Life* (G.Bell & Sons, 1936).

Montmorency's involvement with Cocos Island began in 1898, when he met Captain Palliser (whom he called Shrapnel). Palliser had conceived a plan to hire a steamship in Panama, and sail from there to Cocos. He and another man called Grant set up a syndicate to finance their expedition in the autumn of 1902, which Montmorency joined. The syndicate did a deal with some Liverpool ship owners who wanted to carry cement to the Pacific coast of Mexico, where it was required for the construction of a harbour at the western end of the Trans-Mexican railway. The Liverpudlians bought a steamship called *Scotia* off the Anchor Line which was renamed the *Lytton*. On 1 May 1903 permission was obtained from the Costa Rican ambassador in Paris to search for treasure on Cocos Island for a period of one year, the Costa Ricans to receive one half of all the profits.

The *Lytton* sailed to Swansea (for coal) and Antwerp (for cement). It was decided to hire a Chinese crew and Montmorency (who was an unapologetic racist, like most Europeans at the time) explained why

> Chinamen are more amenable to discipline than Europeans; besides they are cheaper, more hardworking and soberer than the generality of merchant-sailors.

Montmorency had a map of the Island and he also had three detailed 'Clues' or sets of directions: Fitzgerald's, Chapelle's and Flower's, named after three earlier explorers, who had each gone in search of treasure and in some cases claimed to have found it. In addition he had a precise description of the cave where the treasure lay.

> The cave, if found without the door being damaged or blown up, will surprise all who see it, on account of the ingenious contrivance and workmanship, possibly done by Peruvian workers in stone, whose skill was noted. In Keating's words, the cave is between twelve and fifteen feet square, with sufficient standing room. The entrance to it is closed by a stone made to move round in such a peculiar manner that it sets into the rock when you turn it, leaving a passage through which one man can crawl into the cave at a time, and when the stone

is turned back in its place, the human eye cannot detect it; it fits like a paper on a wall. You have to find a hole into which a man's thumb can fit; when you find that mark, insert into it an iron bar, one man can easily turn it. In that cave are gold and silver and images enough to load a vessel.[37]

At this point Montmorency added another fascinating detail to the myth – which was that the treasure entrusted to Thompson included 'the Madonna of Lima'.

> One ship was consigned with the treasures from the Cathedral of Lima, representing centuries of donations to the church. Amongst the cargo was a life-sized statue of the 'Madonna and Child' in pure gold, encrusted with precious stones.[38]

After many hair-raising adventures, Montmorency's party eventually reached Cocos Island. As they approached it, they discussed the various Clues which the leaders had as to the location of the treasure; and they also talked about two alarming cables which they had received. These contained a warning that they would find another British expedition on the Island, which would contest their advance. On the strength of these reports, they decided to land in Chatham Bay under cover of darkness. They made landfall on 9 August 1903, and were immediately struck by the natural beauty of the Island, despite the darkness. They could also see, in the remarkably deep but clear water, large numbers of sharks and enormous 'skates', or rays.

They spent nine exhausting days looking for the treasure, pursuing each of their Clues in turn and trying to match them up; but they found that the landscape had changed somewhat since the Clues had been prepared. This was thought to be because the numerous streams which poured out of the jungle had eroded the earth so quickly. At all events they found nothing.

---

37 Montmorency, 181-2, 76-9.
38 Montmorency, 46; also *From Machu Picchu to Darkest Africa at RGSSA* [the Royal Geographical Society of South Australia: rgssamachupicchu.blogspot.com/2015/09/pirates-of-collection.html

They set sail for Panama, but decided to call in at the next Bay, to the West, round Colnett Point, which was Wafer Bay.

To their surprise, they found some corrugated iron huts there, and a Costa Rican flag. This was all that remained of the small German colony established by August Gissler;[39] but Gissler himself was still there, and he made a deep impression on Montmorency, who thought him 'a man of resource and invention', indeed a modern Robinson Crusoe. Montmorency opined that no-one knew more than Gissler about the treasure of Cocos Island. He had collected every Clue, dug a complex system of tunnels, and sifted every piece of evidence. The German told the newcomer that, although he had found nothing, he was still convinced that he would find treasure, if only he could attract further investment.[40]

Montmorency was not persuaded. He expresses no wish in his book to return to the Island – indeed he says there is little point, in view of Gissler's prolonged search and constant failure; but then, as the late Mandy Rice-Davies once said during the Profumo affair, he would say that, wouldn't he? The reader is left wondering whether Montmorency was holding something back, because in truth, he was not ready to give up just yet.

Montmorency never forgot his journeys to the Pacific. As late as 1936, he wrote to *The Times* from Arthur's Club in S.W.1., on the subject of the eyesight of birds, informing readers that he had 'watched frigate birds for hours at a time in Central America and on Cocos Island.'[41] But, although his account of the expedition of 1903 is entertaining, he was not a historian. He cited no sources except for certain unspecified 'records of Peru', possibly in the national library in Lima, which relate 'the capture, trial and sentence of Thompson and his companions', and the 'researches of Captain Shrapnel'. Other than this, he relied on the fact that 'the Governor of the Lima Bank treasured the traditions of twelve million dollars lost through the piracy of the captain of the *Mary Dear*'; on 'traditions repeated in all the Pacific ports'; and

---

39 For the colony see Hancock & Weston, 113, 305; and chapter 5 below.
40 Gissler's story is related in detail by Hancock & Weston. They had at least some of his papers.
41 *The Times*, 8 January 1936.

on inventions of his own devising (for example, the numerous drawings with which his book is illustrated).[42]

EARL FITZWILLIAM

In 1904, the 7th Earl Fitzwilliam (poosibly the richest man in England) mounted an expedition in conjunction with Admiral Palliser (this being Palliser's third) and a group of friends. The Earl provided miners, mining engineers and a ship, the *Harlech Castle*, which he re-named *Véronique*.[43] The Earl also obtained a concession from the Costa Rican government, while Palliser provided the seamanship and a map, or Clue.

Once in Costa Rica, the Earl's party encountered Montmorency (who was there on his third expedition); and this forced Fitzwilliam to travel up to the capital San José, by railway and donkey, to clarify the terms of his concession with the President of the Republic. This was apparently done, to everyone's satisfaction, and there is no evidence for the story that the Earl's party had a fight with any rival expedition on the Island. However, Fitzwilliam was visited there by Gissler, who initially objected to his presence, but acquiesced once the visit to the President had been explained to him.

Fitzwilliam's men only stayed on Cocos Island for five days, before they blew themselves up with high explosive, whilst trying to remove a landslip which (as they thought) lay in the way of the treasure. The whole party had to retire, nursing their wounded, to Panama. Despite the failure of the expedition, it is clear from Cooke-Yarborough's account that its members would have carried on with their search even now, if Ftizwilliam had permitted it;[44] but he felt that he had put them through enough. Accordingly, he sold the ship and booked separate passages home, for himself and the officers, and the rest of the men.

Fitzwilliam wanted all along to keep his expedition out of the public eye. He swore his friends and the entire crew to secrecy and repeatedly told enquirers that he had gone in search of coal and minerals; but very few believed him,

---

42 Montmorency, 28.
43 TNA BT 110/222/10.
44 Doncaster Archives, the Cooke-Yarborough Collection, DZ/MZ/30/Y1.

and the secrecy only encouraged wild speculation in the British Press. One newspaper published a less than complimentary cartoon, lampooning the Earl and the Admiral, and humorously suggesting that his activities might start a 'society craze' for treasure-hunting.

In Fitzwilliam's estate village of Wentworth, in the West Riding of Yorkshire, the miners who had accompanied him kept their word, and never spoke to anyone about the treasure-hunt; but two of Fitzwilliam's friends wrote accounts of the voyage of the *Véronique*. Eustace Cooke-Yarborough never published his; but David's Smith's, entitled *El Dorado*, appeared in *Blackwood's Magazine* in 1932, also the year in which Campbell's *My Greatest Adventure* was published.[45]

THE TWO LADIES

Another British expedition set off in 1912 under Miss L. Brocklesby Davis and Mrs. Barre Tile (or Till), who had a concession for two years. The stated purpose of the expedition was to raise funds for charity;[46] but a note of scepticism was sounded by the *Dundee Evening Telegraph* for 3 July 1911.

MRS B. TILE GOES IN SEARCH
Of Pirates' Hoard of Jewels and Gold
WHICH SHE HOPES TO DEVOTE TO CHARITY

> The treasure hunters are at work again. Mrs B. Tile, a London philanthropist, has gone to Cocos Island to discover the Pirates' Hoard. The party, equipped for a ten week's stay, includes Miss Davis (London) and two Englishmen, Messrs E. S. Macintosh and F. Biekerson. It is Mrs Tile's intention to devote the find - when it is found - to charitable work in London, where she has been identified with "Welfare" organisations for many years.

---

45 See E.F.T.I. (2016)
46 H.M.S.O., 21 (with references to *The Times South American Supplement* and *The Times* itself.

El Dorado

The hidden gold on Island, which is in the iris blue bay of Panama, and under the sovereignty of Costa Rica, is an old, old story with plenty of chapters—in fact, until the glittering treasure is located it may be safely prophesied that there will not be end to them. So much romance has been woven round the Cocos Island that it as well to set forth the truth about it. The buried wealth is in two parts; one consists of jewels and boxes of gold belonging to the burgesses of Callao, and the other is the pillage and loot from South American towns plundered by Benito Bonito and his cutthroat crew.

Chase of the *Mary Dear*

In 1825 [sic] the people of Callao, anticipating a raid by filibusters, bargained with Captain Thomson [sic], of the British barque *Mary Dear*, to husband the wealth of their city on his ship. When all the treasure was aboard he murdered the guards and sailed for a then rocky waste off ships' track called the Cocos Island, which of old had been a haunt of buccaneers. They landed eleven boatloads of priceless valuables and placed them in a cache.

The Peruvians pursued the *Mary Dear*, captured the crew, and hanged them, sparing only Thomson and his mate on condition that they disclosed the cache. The two, however, escaped, and Thomson joined Benito Bonito the buccaneer, and they hid a vast store of pillage and gold from Acapulco on the Cocos. Before they could return for it a British man-of-war captured the pirate vessel, and Thomson again saved his skin. He and a Frenchman named Chapelle escaped hanging by turning king's evidence.

Now Cocos Island is not in the bay of Panama, nor anywhere near it; and the Peruvian Revolution took place in 1821 not 1825. Moreover, the term 'filibuster' is an anachronism for the events of the 1820s, since it originally referred to those, like Drake, who raided Spanish colonies and ships in the West Indies, and was later applied to citizens of the U.S.A. who fomented insurrections in Texas and Nicaragua. Lastly, this is the first time we have seen it suggested that Thompson (or Thomson's) career, as a companion of the notorious pirate Benito Bonito, postdated his seizure of the treasure of Lima/Callao, rather than preceded it.

But, to return to the two British ladies, we learn more from a report in the *Exeter and Plymouth Gazette* for 13 July 1912.

TREASURE HUNT
LADY LEADERS
FRESH EXPEDITION TO COCOS ISLANDS
£20,000,000 GOLD AND JEWELS

Another expedition is about to start in quest of the Spanish treasure said to have been hidden by pirates on the lonely island of Cocos, off the Spanish Main. Years have elapsed since gold and jewels to the value twenty million pounds were seized from the Jesuits when they were expelled from Peru, and taken from Spanish treasure by old-time buccaneers. This fabulous wealth, so it is said, was deposited on Cocos Island, where it has remained to this day safe in a secret hoard.

A syndicate has been formed to attempt to recover the treasure, and a steamer, the *Melmore*, formerly engaged in the Great Railway Company's cross-Channel service, has been secured. She has a speed of about ten knots, and is now at Plymouth preparing for sea. She is expected to leave within a few days for Barry to coal, and will proceed thence, via the Straits of Magellan, up the coast to Panama. There she will be joined by two ladies, who are among the principals of the expedition.

These were on Cocos Island last year, when they are stated to have been successful in locating the exact whereabouts of the cave where the treasure was concealed. They made drawings of the spot, and brought plans to England, which are now at the disposal of the present syndicate. The ladies have already left London for Panama. Their names are given as Mrs. Barry Till and Miss Davis.

The exact date of the departure of the latest Cocos Island expedition from Plymouth, says the *Pall Mall Gazette*, has not been fixed, but six weeks at sea should suffice to see the *Melmore* at Cocos. A concession has been obtained from the Costa Rica Government. A new feature of the expedition is the inclusion of cinematograph operators, that the public may have reproduced the efforts to recover the treasure.

The inaccuracies here are not hard to detect. First the journalist is entirely unclear as to which island or islands he is referring to, perhaps because he is confusing Cocos Island in the Pacific with the Cocos (Keeling) Islands. Second, Cocos Island is not, and never was, in 'the Spanish Main', which was confined to the Caribbean and Gulf of Mexico. Third, this is the first and only time it has ever been suggested that any of the treasure taken to Cocos Island was stolen 'from the Jesuits when they were expelled from Peru.' The Jesuits were indeed expelled from Spain and her Latin American possessions as a whole, in 1767;[47] but this was 25 years before any pirates are known to have operated off the coast of Costa Rica and Panama, and 50 years before the Peruvian Revolution of 1821.

This second expedition was not a success. A terse report appeared in both *The Scotsman* and the *Aberdeen Press and Journal* on 25 February 1913.

TREASURE HUNT IN COCOS ISLAND

PANAMA, February 24. The treasure-hunting party from Plymouth, led by Mrs Barry Till and Miss Genevieve Davis, which has been searching Cocos Island, in the Pacific, for treasure supposed to have been buried there by pirates and others many years ago, has arrived

---

47   *The Jesuits in Latin America*, Jeffrey Klaiber, S.J., http://www.internationalbuetin.org/issues/2004-02/2004-02-063.

on board the steamer *Melmore*. They have brought no treasure back with them.[48]

However, ridiculous as the enterprise might now seem – and perhaps the whole idea of women explorers seemed ridiculous in 1911 and 1912 – the two ladies were not willing to give up, even now. The *Evening Telegraph and Post* for 28 May 1913 reported as follows.

LOST TREASURE
ENGLISH EXPEDITION
To Cocos Island a Failure

The fourth English company that has attempted to recover the Cooos Island treasure within the past seven years has returned to Panama unsuccessful, and its ship is for sale, says the Panama correspondent of *The Times*. This last expedition was undertaken by two Englishwomen and a few men employees.

Company Formed

They returned to London, and there interested a number of EngJish businessmen, among them, and at the head of the project, E. C. Evelyn Mills, a hardware merchant. A company was formed with enough funds to fit out a ship of 500 tons to continue the search. The ship was supplied with provisions for a six months' voyage, and great steel boxes with special locks were built into the hull for the safe storage of the treasure.

Failure

Some months ago the ship sailed, and, going around South America, reached Cocos Island. Five months later it came into the entrance

---

48 See also the more amusing report in the *Sheffield Evening Telegraph* for 14 March 1913.

of the Panama Canal, and the owners offered it for sale. The search had been a failure. Mr Mills is no longer a believer in the clue and the story of the pirate's treasure. Since the treasure was buried in the cave in the cliff there have been great slides of rock and earth along the front of the island, and these have completely covered the spot to which the magnetic bearings specified in the clue point. The women are returning to London intent upon organising another company for the purpose of continuing the search.

One might think that the myths had now been exposed for what they were; and it seems that this was certainly the conclusion of the hardware merchant Mills; but it was evidently not the conclusion reached by Miss Davis and Mrs Tile. Nor is there much sign of any widespread disillusionment among the treasure-hunting community in Britain. None of the British adventurers who went out in the 1890s and early 1900s had found anything, but they were not put off by this lack of success, any more than they were by disconcerting encounters with rivals, extreme weather, and misadventure. Nor does it seem that their hopes were crushed by the sceptical tone taken by some British newspapers, and by Chetwood and Paine in their books, published in 1904 and 1911.[49] Many of them would have gone back if they had been given the opportunity. Moreover, although the outbreak of a World War in 1914 put an end to treasure-hunting on Cocos Island, the interruption proved only temporary. Interest revived when peace returned; and as we shall see, the British Foreign Office did not treat the myths surrounding Cocos Island as unworthy of belief.

---

49 See chapter 4 below.

Chapter 4

AMERICAN ADVENTURERS

When California became a state of the Union in 1850, the U.S.A. had only 31 states, and a population of 17 millions; but by 1900 there were 45 states and 76 million people. Commerce, industry and agriculture had all exploded, making the country a rival to Great Britain and Imperial Germany. The late 19th century saw the advent of electric lighting, telephones, phonographs, typewriters, the internal combustion engine, and many other inventions.

In 1854 the Cocos Island Treasure Company was founded in San Francisco, with a capital investment of $550,000. This company proceeded to promote many voyages to the Island between 1854 and 1869, though we have few details.[50] The U.S.A. (and particularly southern Caifornia) is a lot nearer to Cocos Island than is Great Britain; and the journey for Americans living on the Pacific coast was incomparably shorter than it was for the British, even before the completion in 1914 of the Panama Canal, which facilitated voyages from the eastern seaboard. It is therefore likely that, in the century and half before treasure-hunting was finally prohibited, more Americans travelled to Cocos Island than the British; and some of these clearly did so before Robert

---

50 Knobloch, 169.

Louis Stevenson visited California in 1880. Treasure stories were being told up and down the Pacific coast long before then.

EARLY AMERICAN LEGENDS

In his book *La Isla del Coco* (1992) Christopher Weston told how an Englishman living in California, discovered some letters, already old and yellow, in 1898. These told a story about the American filibusters, who travelled to various parts of Central America to foment revolution in the 1850s.

[The letters] were found in the dusty attic of an old house that was demolished in "Barrio Otoya" in San José, telling a story about how a group of recruits who had joined William Walker in Nicaragua in his daring adventure to try and dominate Central America, had sailed to Cocos Island in 1856 just after Walker's troops were defeated by the Costa Ricans...

The letters also told how, after their defeat, the mercenaries fled from Nicaragua aboard one of Cornelius Vanderbilt's clipper ships, which they had captured in the Port of San Juan del Sur early in May, 1856. Sailing to Cocos Island, they anchored in Chatham Bay, and a scouting party which rowed over to Wafer Bay found a huge cave located on the northern tip of Isla Nuez.

> The tide was low, and as they approached the big square entrance to the cave in search of a supply of molluscs to take aboard their ship, they saw a huge bronze chain anchored to the rocky and jagged floor of the cave and running into the ocean from its mouth. The ten men were able to get a foothold on several of the nearby rocks, after approaching with their longboat, and they managed to pull the very heavy bronze chain up out of the sea, to find that there was a large iron chest securely bolted to the end. The filibusters, after much effort and strain, were able to get the heavy chest into their boat, and took it back to their ship anchored in the middle of the bay, much to the surprise of their shipmates.

After opening the chest, the fortunate men found it full to the brim of shining gold doubloons from the Lima mint in Peru.

A few years later, on 29 November 1869, the *Glasgow Herald* ran the following story.

> Your readers will remember the story concerning 10,000,000 dollars in silver buried on the Cocos Island, which was started in San Francisco ten years ago, and has been probably published in every country newspaper in the United States. The tale was that a doctor in San Francisco was one night called to the bedside of a sick and poverty-stricken sailor. The doctor watched over him carefully [but] in spite of all his precautions the sailor grew worse…
>
> On his dying bed, with tears in his eyes, he thanked the doctor for all his kindness, and said that he could and would repay him for all his trouble. In a few short breaths he told him that in his younger days he had been a pirate. With twenty companions he had shipped at Callao on a Spanish treasure ship bound to Cadiz. When five days out they rose and butchered the officers and passengers, after which the course of the ship was changed due west. Three weeks afterwards during a drunken carousal, the ship ran upon a reef of rocks fringing an island in the Pacific, and before morning eight of the buccaneers were drowned. At the break of day they reached the shore in boats, and found the island fertile and pleasant. After three days' hard work, they brought the kegs of silver dollars to the shore, and buried them. The treasure amounted to over 10,000,000 dollars…
>
> At the conclusion of his story the dying sailor drew from under his bolster a roll of papers giving the latitude and longitude of the island as near as possible… A careful study of the chart located the island in the vicinity of Cocos. The doctor embarked in the scheme with all his wealth, rigged out a schooner, and sailed from San Francisco in search of the El Dorado. He returned a ruined

man, unable to discover the island. Other expeditions were fitted out, but none were successful.

In July, 1868, several gentlemen in this city bought a schooner and fitted out an expedition. They reached the island after fifty-six days' navigation, thoroughly worn out and disgusted. They spent nineteen days there vainly looking for the hidden riches, and then gave up the hunt as entirely Utopian.

Last winter some of the superstitious and wealthy citizens of Costa Rica began to agitate the subject anew. A company was organised, composed of some of the prominent Government officials. They left Costa Rica in June last. Nothing has been heard of them until yesterday, when a letter was received from one of the party by a friend in this city, containing intelligence of the discovery of the treasure.

It is to be noted that in none of these stories is there any mention of Captain Thompson or the *Mary Dear.* Nor is there any reference to Keating of Newfoundland, though he was supposed to have made the first of his voyages in 1844; and, there is no mention of Fitzgerald either. There is a brief mention, in the last of them, of the Peruvian Revolution; but the tone of this Panama correspondent is distinctly sceptical. However, we cannot say this of the next correspondent, who called himself 'Old Panama' and wrote to the editor of the *Glasgow Herald* soon afterwards, with yet another version of the legend.

"SIR During the years in which Spain was trying to I bring her revolutionary colonists in North and South America again under control, a band of pirates, in command of a well armed and fast sailing brig, were engaged in pillaging the coast towns along the Gulf of Mexico and the Spanish Main.

The Rosa, for such was one of the names of this saucy craft, became the depository of a very valuable collection of gold and silver ornaments, jewels, precious stones and money. The Caribbean Sea, hot as it always is, was also becoming, in another sense, too hot for them... Having rounded the "'Horn," they set fairly to work, and whilst coasting along the sea board of Chili [sic], Peru, Ecuador, and New Grenada...

Having reached as far north as Panama Bay, the Cocos Islands [sic] were selected for their purpose... A council was held and a division of the spoil made into two portions - one of them named "the general good" and the other the "crew's portion." This arrangement being completed, the treasure was conveyed from the Rosa to the shore...

The "general good" portion of the treasure, as far as the writer knows, has not been found (although he believes the crew's portion has), and he has no doubt that it still exists, and will ultimately be discovered. I have only to add that the man already referred to, who died in Costa Rica, said on his deathbed that he only knew one other man to be alive who knew as much as he did on the subject, and that the man to whom he referred is known to have died some years ago."

This article was written to correct the previous article; but it only adds to the general confusion, because it confuses Cocos Island in the Pacific with the Cocos (Keeling) Islands in the Indian Ocean. Moroever, although 'Old Panama' does refer to the disorder arising from the wars for independence from Spain, his pirates are not Captain Thompson & Co; and the ship is called the *Rosa*, not *Mary Dear*, or any variant of that name. Having said that it is interesting that Old Panama already refers to the existence of many different versions of the story.

THE 'GOOD OLD INDIAN'
A report in the *Dundee Evening Telegraph* for 11 November 1897 started with the Palliser story; but continued with something quite different, and with a strongly American flavour.

THE REPORTED TREASURE ISLAND
A BUBBLE OF MUCH ENDURANCE

The other day a Vancouver correspondent of a daily paper gravely cabled that there was no truth in the reported discovery by Her Majesty's ship *Impérieuse* of a vast treasure on Cocos Island. A party from the vessel the island but failed to discover the treasure, the existence which is highly doubtful.

From the time the learned and enterprising buccaneer Dampier to the present day Cocos Island has been visited time and again by expeditions to discover the vast hoard treasure supposed to have been buried there when Morgan and his kind harried and burned the Spanish towns the Pacific and Atlantic sides of Central America. Twenty-six years ago the writer sailed with a Scandinavian sailor in one of Tour de Wolf's trading schooners in the South Seas. This man, Andrew Larson, had formed one of the members of an expedition that sailed from San Francisco in 1866 to

UNEARTH THE BURIED TREASURE ON COCOS ISLAND

His account of the inception of the venture was exceedingly humorous. A Company was formed on the strength of the statement of an old Indian, native of the Gulf of San Miguel, the Isthmus of Panama. The aged Indian, it appeared, was deeply grateful to the captain of an American sperm whaler, who had cured his "only and beautiful daughter of deadly fever," and desirous to make the blubber-hunting skipper some return for his medicinal offices, he showed him some "old documents written in English and Spanish that denoted the exact situation on the Cocos Islands where thirty millions of gold and silver money had been hidden by the old-time buccaneers." Strange as it may appear, there were people in San Francisco who "bit" the bait. Ten thousand dollars were raised at once, and

THIRTY TREASURE HUNTERS

who wanted to dig the hidden gold and silver coin contributed another ten thousand. A schooner was chartered and fitted out, and here the enterprising whaling captain who had inaugurated the enterprise withdrew and went home to Martha's vineyard with £2000 his jacket. The good old Indian, however, in a moment of inebriety, confessed to the leader of the expedition that he

WASN'T AN INDIAN ALL

but a native of Honolulu, in the Sandwich Islands, also that he had no daughter and knew nothing about any treasure anywhere. But the treasure-seekers, not knowing this, sailed nevertheless. They reached the Cocos Island and dug away most manfully, but got nothing but fever; and after five weeks' labour met and solemnly cursed the venerable Indian person as fraud.

Now it is clear that this writer was a sceptic, and denounced the expedition which sailed out of San Francisco in 1866 as a scam; but the interesting thing from our point of view is that, once again, in this early American version of the legend, there is no Thompson, no *Mary Dear*, and not even a treasure of Lima. On this occasion, the treasure which the fraudsters sold to the gullible was treasure which had been supposedly buried on Cocos by Captain Morgan (c. 1635-1688) – in other words, a pirate from the classic buccaneering period of the 17th century (recently recommended by Dr Liam Fox as a model for modern British businessmen, post-'Brexit'). True, reference is made to the year 1821, and to a 'London privateer'; but the story bears no resemblance to the legendary escapades of Captain William Thompson in Peru.

THE *VANDERBILT*

The following report, which appeared in the Hemel *Hempstead Gazette and West Herts Advertiser* for 6 December 1879, relates once more to an American expedition.

The *San Francisco Call* of October 31 says "Cocos Island, situated off the coast of Central America, is popularly supposed to be thickly planted with bags of treasure. Expeditions have several times gone in search of these mythical millions, but have fcnd none. The schooner *Vanderbilt*, which sailed from this port on the 12th of April last, arrived at Santa Barbara a week ago with a discouraged, goldless crew. For three months they toiled upon the beach under a tropical sun, digging for buried gold, running tunnels and drifts, and sinking pits, and ditches; but their labour was in vain."[51]

It was perhaps no accident that the *Vanderbilt* was named after Cornelius Vanderbilt (1794 – 1877), an American tycoon who built his wealth in railroads and shipping, and was regarded by Eric Hobsbawm as one of the original 'robber barons' of American history.[52]

'JAMES BRAWN'

The next story relates to a voyage which, unlike some of those referred to here, is very well documented. The following report of it appeared in the *Derry Journal* on 11 September 1903.

THE LATEST TREASURE ISLAND
A FASCINATING SPORT

The latest attempt to find the rich treasure of gold, silver, and jewels reported to be buried Cocos Island, in the Pacific, has ended, like the others, in failure, The treasure island is less than 500 miles southwest of Panama, its exact position being lat. 5.32.57N., and long. 86.58.22 W.

The schooner *Herman*, with an American expedition which has been searching for several millions in Chilian gold alleged to buried

---

51 See also Knobloch, 172-3.
52 Hobsbawm, *Age of Capital*.

on Cocos or some other South Pacific island, has abandoned the search. The treasure-seekers searched twenty islands, and then the originator of the scheme confessed that he was ignorant of the locality of the treasure island.

In fact this was a highly inaccurate and incomplete account of the voyage in question, which (paradoxically) was not made with the aim of going to Cocos Island at all. The full story is told by John Chetwood in his book *Our Search for the Missing Millions of Cocos Island* (1904). Chetwood explains that he and five other Americans had set out from San Francisco in 1902, and that they did not even land on Cocos Island, let alone spend any time searching for treasure there. Instead, they visited various islands in the South Pacific, including Penrhyn in the Northern group of the Cook Islands, Papeete in French Polynesia, and Flint Island in the Central Pacific, all of which are over 2,000 miles from Costa Rica.

The reason the *Herman* made this extraordinary journey was that one of the crew had recently met a Captain James Brawn [sic], now an old man, in San Francisco. Brawn had told him how, as a young man, he had known one Captain Schmidt, whose father had 'carried away and concealed' an immense amount of gold and silver from Callao in 1820, 'on the eve of a threatened bombardment of the city by a Spanish fleet', and buried it on Cocos Island.

Supposedly, Schmidt senior was unable to return to Cocos Island to recover his ill-gotten gains. Instead, it fell to his son and to Brawn to return there in 1850. They found the treasure and took it away a second time, on board the *Black Witch*, re-burying it on another remote island in the South Pacific. Given time and money, Brawn said he could find this second island again, and show his listeners where the treasure was located.

At this point, Chetwood tells us that he at least was very dubious. In particular, he thought there was probably more than one treasure still on Cocos Island, and it was unlikely that the British Government would have sent Admiral Palliser there to look for it, if this had not been so. (In fact, of course, there is no evidence that Palliser was on official business when he landed on Cocos Island in 1897). However, Chetwood and his fellows ran a check on Brawn and, surprisingly, decided that they would invest in his wild idea. They even formed a limited company – Cocos Island Treasure Search Expedition Ltd – to raise money for the purpose; and set off.

The rest is predictable. The *Herman* called in on numerous islands in the South and Central Pacific, before Brawn admitted that he could not remember where he and Schmidt junior had buried the treasure. Subjected to 'imprecations' and threats of prosecution for fraud, he remembered some bits of information and took his companions to Flint Island; but, once there, he was unable to tell them where they should dig. The expedition ran out of money, and the adventurers returned to Tahiti, where they sold the *Herman* to help pay their debts, before returning in disappointment to California. Chetwood seriously thought of prosecuting Brawn; but contented himself with the inclusion of two mottoes at the start of his book:

'Honesty is the best policy'

'All that glitters is not gold'

Even this was not the last of Schmidt and Brawn. They re-appeared in disguise in a Californian newspaper in 1909, seven years after the return of the *Herman* and five years after the publication of Chetwood's book.

CAPTAIN JAMES BROWN'S STORY OF BURIED TREASURE

The following account of the famous treasure supposed to have been buried on Cocos Island, and the object of so many adventurous expeditions, was dictated last night and signed by Captain James Brown [sic], who leaves today for the South Seas to recover the treasure trove.

In the year 1850 I shipped on board a vessel in New York as second mate for the West Indies. Arriving at Kingston, Jamaica, I became acquainted with Captain Henry Smith of the schooner *Sea Foam*, 400 tons register, who was there fitting out for pearl fishing, and I joined his vessel as chief mate. After being at sea for some time the captain told me what his real business consisted of, which was that we were to go to Cocos Island after treasure which had been buried there by his father.

Then he told me about his father, Captain Smith, of the schooner *Black Witch* of Salem, Mass. He was on the coast of Peru when the Spaniards were fighting that country in 1820, and came in contact with their vessels from which he took all their treasure, amounting to about $60,000,000, and consisting of silver, silver dollars, gold bars, bullion and gold and silver jewels from the churches, also diamonds and other precious stones, all of which were taken to Cocos Island and buried.

Before Captain Smith died he imparted the secret to his son, with whom I was now connected. We arrived at Cocos Island and found the treasure and moved it to another island in the South Pacific, where we again buried it. *Captain James Brown.*[53]

Now there are remarkable similarities here with the story told by John Chetwood about the voyage of the *Herman*; but Schmidt has become Smith; and Brown has become Brawn. The main events are supposed to have taken place around 1820. We also hear once more of Cocos Island and of the Peruvian Revolution. However, there is no mention of Captain Thompson and his brig, nor of Keating. In addition, we cannot help remarking that, if James Brown (or Brawn) had taken part in his first voyage in search of treasure in 1850, and then accompanied the crew of the *Herman* in 1902, and was still alive and well and keen to embark on a further voyage in 1909, he must have been a very fit man for his age.[54]

---

53 *San Francisco Call*, 2 February 1909.
54 For more on James Brown, see Nesmith, 230-4.

DESBOROUGH

The San Francisco *Call* for 2 February 1909 contained the following story:

LOS ANGELES MAN ASSERTS KNOWLEDGE OF $17,000,000 BURIED ON COCOS ISLAND TELLS WEIRD TALE OF HIDDEN GOLD

Los Angeles, Feb. 6. Convinced that he can locate and recover treasure to the amount of $17,000,000, supposed to have been buried on Cocos Island, 350 miles off the Costa Rica coast, W. A. Desborough of Los Angeles is about to embark for the tropic seas in search of the vast fortune.

Desborough says he knows nothing of the proposed expedition of Captain Brown, who wrote the statement printed in the *Call,* Feb. 2nd, and does not think they are after the same treasure. Desborough says he was on the island eleven years ago, but did little more than to locate the cache where the money was hidden. He declares it is buried by a landslide and lies beneath a quantity of earth forty feet deep, and as large as a city block. It is his purpose to raise enough money to take hydraulic machinery to uncover the treasure.

Desborough's story of how the treasure came to be buried there sounds very much like a sea yarn. In speaking of it later, he said:

"In the war between Chile and Peru in the middle of the last century, the people of Callao became alarmed by rumors of an attack on the city. They took all their treasure aboard the bark *Mary Deane* of Boston. The captain's cupidity was aroused and he sailed away with the treasure, which he cached on Cocos Island. The bark was overtaken by a Peruvian man-of-war and all the crew, excepting the captain and the mate, were slain. These men escaped after awful torture; they swam to an American whaler and were at sea eighteen months. The mate died and the captain returned to Boston.

I obtained possession of the chart from a daughter of the captain, whom I had befriended. Eleven years ago I visited the place with an expedition but for private reasons did not disclose the correct hiding place. While the men were working at the wrong place I located the treasure and we left the island."

Here we do see a link between the British and American legends: this is the reference to a treasure taken out of the port of Lima by a 'bark' called *Mary Deane* of Boston 'in the war between Chile and Peru in the middle of [the 19th century]'. However, the captain in question is not named and presumably this bark was an American vessel, sailing out of Boston Massachusetts rather than Boston in Lincolnshire. Further, although there was a war between Chile and Peru in 1879, this had nothing to do with the wars of independence, which took place over half a century earlier.

RALPH DELAHAYE PAINE, 1911

1911 saw the publication of *The Book of Buried Treasure* by Ralph Delahaye Paine (1871 – 1925). Paine was a prolific and popular American journalist and author, who led a life of adventure and then held several government offices. His book is well-researched and has a wide focus; but Chapter Ten deals with 'The Lure of Cocos Island'. [55]

Paine places the central event event in 1820 rather than 1821.

> The versions of this story agree in the essential particular that it was Captain Thompson of the merchant brig *Mary Dear* who stole the twelve million dollars' worth of plate, jewels, and gold coin which had been entrusted to him by the Spanish residents of Lima in 1820, and buried them on Cocos Island.

Thompson's relationship with Keating is dealt with as follows.

---

55   11 November 1911 also saw the publication of an article in *The Newburgh Telegram* (Newburgh, N.Y.) by Walter Noble Burns (1866-1932) entitled *The Treasure of Cocos Island [etc]* which referred the principal character as 'Bugs' Thompson, and tells us that he absconded with the Treasure in 1838.

> It is related that a native of Newfoundland, Keating by name, while sailing from England in 1844, met a man of middle age, "handsome in appearance and having about him something of an air of mystery which had an attraction of its own." This was, of course, none other than Captain Thompson of the *Mary Dear*. He became friendly with Keating and when they landed at Newfoundland, the latter asked him to accept the hospitality of his home.
>
> Keating believed the strange tale and passed it on to a ship-owner who agreed to furnish a vessel provided one Captain Bogue should go in command of the expedition. While preparations were under way, Thompson was inconsiderate enough to die, but it goes without saying that he left a map carefully marked with crosses and bearings. Keating and Bogue set sail with this precious document, and after a long and tedious voyage into the Pacific, they cast anchor off Cocos Island.

It will be seen that Paine's tone is sceptical, which is refreshing when so many writers are so credulous. At the same time, it is interesting to see that he purveyed an essentially British version of events to an American audience.

Paine's discussion of British activities on Cocos Island in the 1890s would seem to be based on Montmorency's account, though he does not seem to have realised that, when Montmorency referred to Shrapnel and H.M.S. *Haughty*, he really meant Palliser and H.M.S. *Impérieuse*.

> Herr Gissler was visited in 1896 by Captain Shrapnel of H.M.S. *Haughty* who had heard the stories of Thompson and Benito Bonito along the coastwise ports. By way of giving his blue-jackets something to do, he landed a party three hundred strong on Cocos Island whose landscape they vainly blasted and otherwise disarranged for several days, but without success.

Paine went on to relate the partnership of Palliser and Earl Fitzwilliam in 1904-5; but his account shows how quickly and easily facts can become distorted.

> At that time, a wealthy British naval officer, Lord Fitzwilliam, was bound out to Cocos Island in his own steam yacht with a costly equipment of machinery and a heavy crew to find the treasure. He found poor Gissler in a Costa Rican port, became interested in his wrongs, and promptly supported his claims.
>
> Lord Fitzwilliam took him on board the yacht and in this dignified fashion Gissler returned to this kingdom.
>
> Lord Fitzwilliam and his yacht arrived at Cocos in December of 1904, and the party of laborers fell to with prodigious zest. While they were making the dirt fly, another English expedition, commanded by Arnold Gray, hove in sight, and proceeded to begin excavating at inconveniently close range. In fact, both parties were cocksure that the lost cave was located in one spot beneath a great mass of debris that had tumbled down from the overhanging height. The inevitable result was that a pretty quarrel arose. Neither force would yield its ground.
>
> The climax was a pitched battle in which heads were broken and considerable blood spilt.

In fact, Fitzwilliam was an army office, not a naval officer. More importantly, it is not true that took Gissler back to Cocos Island at the end of 1904. In fact, the Earl's party found Gissler on the Island when they landed. Nor is it true that they encountered Arnold Gray's expedition there, though they had encountered Montmorency's on the mainland. Nor was there any kind of fight on the island, such as Paine describes.[56]

Paine closes his account with this reflective passage.

> Since [1905] hardly a year has passed but an expedition or two for Cocos Island has been in the wind... To enumerate these ventures and describe them in detail would make a tiresome catalogue of the names of vessels and adventurous men with the treasure bee in their

---

56 See Cooper & Moorhouse, *Earl Fitzwilliam's Treasure Island* (2016) for the Cooke-Yarborough account, which is held by Doncaster Archives.

bonnets. Charts and genuine information are no longer necessary to one of these expeditions. Cocos Island is under such a spell as has set a multitude to digging for the treasure of Captain Kidd. The gold is there, this is taken for granted, and no questions are asked. The island was long a haunt of buccaneers and pirates, this much is certain, and who ever heard of a true pirate of romance who knew his business that did not employ his spare time in "a-burying of his treasure?"

Chapter 5

THE GERMAN EXPERIMENT

August Gissler (1858-1935) was the first man to live on Cocos Island on a permanent basis, and indeed he lived on it longer than anyone has ever done - for eighteen years on and off, between 1890 and 1908. During that time, the Costa Ricans appointed him its one and only Governor, and he established a short-lived colony. The truly extraordinary thing is that he was German, as were all the colonists. This does make one wonder whether there was something more at work here than one man's personal obsession with buried treasure.

Gissler's history has been written from two different points of view – his own and the Costa Rican. Hancock & Julian Weston's book *The Lost Treasure of Cocos Island* (1960) was based on his diaries, letters and other papers, which came into their possession some time after his death. Christopher Weston's *La Isla del Coco* (1992) drew on the same materials, but it also on others unknown to his father Julian, in particular Agustin Guido's account of the Costa Rican expedition made in 1905.[57] It was written from a Costa Rican point of view, by someone who was principally interesting in diving and in the natural

---

[57] According to Weston this was first published in a review of the *Colegio Superior de Señoritas* (San José, Costa Rica) for the months of July and August 1935: C.Weston, 110.

treasures of Cocos Island, for whom treasure-hunting was a thing of the past. For Gissler, the treasure was a lifelong obsession.

※

Gissler first went to sea in 1880. On a long voyage he met a young Portuguese named Manoel Cabral, who told him about his grandfather's career as a pirate on board a vessel called *Le Renard*. These pirates had captured a brig, which they re-named the *Relampago*, which (acccording to Montmorency) was the same name as that borne by a vessel which had once belonged to the pirate Benito Bonito. Cabral's *Relampago* captured a Spanish vessel carrying much bullion, called *Rosario*, somewhere between in the Pacific between Valparaiso and Acapulco. Having done so, the pirates took their loot to a small island called 'La Palma', and hid it there.

It is clear from the description of 'La Palma', that this was Cocos Island - after all, 'Cocos' is Spanish for coconut, and coconuts grow on palm trees; and, according to Hancock and Weston, it was this reference to the Island which changed Gissler's life. So inspired was he by Cabral's story – and by the map he produced - that Gissler decided then and there to spend to devote his life to the pursuit of the treasure which he was sure lay buried there. However, it is clear from the outset that he was following a different trail from the one followed by the Britons Thompson, Keating and Fitzgerald (and for that matter from the one which led through the American James Alexander Forbes I – see below). Further, the treasure he sought was not the Treasure of Lima. In Cabral's version of the story, there is no mention whatever of the Peruvian Revolution. Cabral's treasure was the result of a different episode, or episodes, in the history of piracy.

Gissler next went to live in Hawaii, where he made friends with a man called Bartels, whose father in law, 'Old Mac', told him that, as early as 1851, he had heard stories of how there was treasure on an island off the west coast of Central America, and he had set off to reach it.[58] He never did, and instead spent some years in Baja California, Mexico, before returning to Hawaii. Old

---

58 C.Weston, 123-4.

Mac had subsequently tried to embark on another treasure-seeking voyage but had been put off by the violent nature of the captain who offered to take him to Cocos; but he had retained both a chart and 'detailed plans' which showed where the treasure could be found.

Bartels and Gissler became convinced that what Old Mac told them was authentic. They compared Old Mac's map with Cabral's and concluded that they pointed to the same place. They decided to go in search of the treasure themselves, especially after the old man revealed that

> The captain he knew by the name of Benito had taken a Spanish galleon off Acapulco, Mexico, and had sailed to Cocos Island and buried the treasure there. But before he could remove it again the captain and his pirate crew were caught by a British man-of-war and all hands with the exception of two men called Chapelle and Thompson were hanged.[59]

At this point there seems to be a confluence of myths. Here was Old Mac of Hawaii telling a tale which resembled in some respects the story told by the informants of British adventurers; but there were many questions which might have been asked. Most importantly, were 'Thompson' and 'Chapelle' the same people as had once allegedly crewed the *Mary Dear*? Gissler appears not to have asked these questions, or to have been aware of the discrepancies. At any rate, he resolved to engage in some serious excavation of his own. Accordingly, he formed a syndicate of 14 men and they chartered the *Wilhelmina*, a small barque of 350 tons, which arrived in sight of Cocos Island in February 1889.

Gissler found it very difficult to land but eventually managed to do so, in Wafer Bay (whereas Palliser, Montmorency and Fitzwilliam all landed in Chatham Bay a few years later). This indicates that the German was not especially interested in the Treasure of Lima, or indeed had never heard of it. As in other fields, British and German goals were different; and this was confirmed by the journalist who interviewed Gissler for the *New York Times* in 1907:

---

59 H & W, 101; C.Weston, 124.

> Cocos Island has figured in many a strange romance of lost treasures. Montezuma's billions are said to be buried there, instead of in Southern Mexico, or Guatemala, and numerous expeditions have been fitted out with a view to finding the gold. In olden times there was a heavy trade between Central America and the Philippines, and ships following the equatorial "counter current" had to pass Cocos. Tradition says vessels laden with precious metals were wrecked on the island and adventurers from many lands have undertaken in vain to find the buried cargoes.[60]

The reference to Montezuma is interesting, because we have previously seen references linking Cocos Island with the Incas, but this is the first time it has been linked with the Aztecs. However, the more important point is that there is no mention here of the Madonna, or Treasure, of Lima, or of the crew of the *Mary Dear*. Gissler seems to have thought that the treasure or treasures which lay hidden on Cocos Island came from the sea, rather than from the land, and were the fruits of the purest piracy, rather than the result of civil war and revolution. In addition, we should note that Hancock & Weston tell us that Gissler only received a copy of Patrick Fitzgerald's letter to Palliser (which clearly refers to Thompson and Keating) in 1897, which was almost ten years after the German first arrived on the Island.

In 1889, Gissler searched for several weeks, with no success. Eventually, the expedition's supplies ran out, and the *Wilhelmina* returned to the mainland. Gissler and three others stayed and persisted in their search for several more months. They found a note on an old door which said that on 31 January 1884 another German, Captain Schwers of the Steamship *Neko*, had 'found the island uninhabited and taken possession of it in the name of the German Emperor'; but there is no evidence that the German government ever pursued the claim.[61]

Eventually, some members of the original company returned in a different ship and those who had remained on the Island were taken to Chile at the

---

60 H&W, Appendix IV.
61 H&W, 108-112.

end of December 1889; but Gissler was determined to go back. He became convinced that he would succeed in finding the treasure, if only he could set up a colony on the Island, to provide a permanent source of labour and food. Accordingly, in 1891, he obtained a concession from the Costa Rican government, permitting him to bring 50 German families to the Island.[62]

Gissler set out for Germany, where he raised some capital, but then went to San Francisco, where he bought a small sloop named the *Hayseed*, then sailed for Puntarenas in Costa Rica and then to the Island. It seems that he now undertook some excavations; but shortly afterwards, whilst back in Puntarenas, he came across a newspaper cutting from the *New York Herald*, stating that a Mr Young of East Boston had gone to Cocos on an expedition organised in Panama. Gissler travelled to Boston and tracked Young down. Young claimed to be a son-in-law of John Keating, who had discovered the hiding place of the Treasure of Lima in 1846. Gissler did a deal with him; Young contributed a map, Gissler put up $700 and two New York promoters agreed to back the venture.[63]

Now here again is a link between Gissler's long romance with Cocos Island, and the British myth concerning the Treasure of Lima; and we should note that the German seems to have been untroubled by the diversity of stories regarding the treasure he sought. He seems to have seen this as confirmation that there must be some truth in them, somewhere. 'No smoke without fire', as it were.

Gissler set off again, this time from New York on a steamer called *City of Para*. The company comprised ten men; but these did not include Young, who was sick. They travelled to Colon and crossed the Isthmus of Panama, then boarded the Pacific Steamer *Acapulco*. Captain Clerk dropped them off on Cocos Island with some supplies, and even gave them a whaleboat; but the party soon became convinced that Young's information was wrong. After two weeks the Americans were taken off the Island by the Pacific Mail's *San Blas*.[64]

---

62 H&W, 113.
63 C. Weston, 125.
64 H&W, 116-120.

In 1894 Gissler formed the Cocos Island Plantation Company, which was registered in New Jersey; and he sold stock to finance the planting of crops as well as fund further excavations. He was President of the new company and signed a new contract with the Government of Costa Rica, on its behalf,. According to the German, this gave him one-half of the Island, the other to be divided into sections for distribution amongst the settlers. Gissler travelled to Europe again, to raise more capital and more importantly, to recruit the settlers.

Initially, he had some success. The chance of acquiring great wealth was undoubtedly attractive. Others were drawn by the prospect of adventure. Many were Gissler's own friends and acquaintances in Germany. Colonialism was part of the *Zeitgeist*; and this was a time when German settlers were flocking to the United States, as well as to Kaiser Wilhelm II's new overseas territories.

Gissler also got married at this time. Frau Gissler was evidently an adventurous woman herself since, as her husband wrote later,

> [She] went with me to the island where the Pacific Mail Steamer *Costa Rica* landed us on the 13th of December, 1894. We were in all six families. From New York we brought lumber and building materials, provisions and seeds. In Panama we secured tropical plants, chickens, ducks and turkeys. The first thing we did was to build more houses and clear the land to plant cane, bananas, vegetables and coffee.[65]

In February, 1895, the Costa Rican government's steam launch, *Turrialba* visited the island for the first time. With Gissler's help Captain Passmore took a series of soundings and obtained other hydrographic data from which he subsequently made a chart of the island. Gissler chose this occasion to send a letter by the *Turrialba*, telling his friends not to send any more families until he had more accommodation built for them. Nevertheless, he was displeased when four more families and three single men arrived in May, bringing building

---

65 H&W, 120.

materials, lumber and tools, rather than the additional supplies Gissler really needed. He wrote that:

> As no more ships came in, it was not long before we ran short of provisions. One of the settlers fell ill, his limbs became swollen, and soon afterwards he died of dropsy."[66]

The settlers had to work extremely hard in the banana, papaya and coffee plantations, and with the domestic animals. The climate was terrible, the heat and humidity very high, the rain constant. There was little time left to look for gold, after the day's work was done. Gradually they lost heart. Many soon decided that the work was too hard, the life poor, the rewards meagre

When the stores ran low in the Autumn of 1895, Gissler built a boat and sailed to the mainland with three men. Then all three decided they no longer wanted to go back - indeed they were so disenchanted with the Island that they were prepared to leave their wives there and start again on the mainland![67] At around this time, Gissler wrote to his brother-in-law Hermann in Germany

> I worked too hard this year, building nine houses, as well as locks and bridges.... Moltke of Bavaria, where we knew each other, is worthless, too lazy to work and has tried to incite people against me. Steiz has allowed himself to be seduced. Ried was right when he said he was not much good. I had taken Steiz on board the ship [so that he could leave]; but then he said he wanted to stay. Well, I will let him run away. And I will do the same with all those who have caused trouble.

Gissler went to see the new Costa Rican President, Yglesias, who agreed to better terms. As Gissler later explained to Hermann:

> Today I share with you the news that the Government has made a new contract with me. If I have found the treasure by the first of

---

66   H&W, 120-1.
67   C.Weston, 126.

January 1900, I shall be given 3,000 hectares of land on the island as my own property, and each family which has cultivated the soil itself shall have half as much again. And because there are other people who want to look for the treasure, the Government has given me a new Concession. The Government shall have a third of any treasure I find. I must bring new settlers in.... Even if we find nothing, the land is to be ours, and in time that must be worth a lage sum of money...

The new contract stipulated that the *Turrialba* should proceed from Costa Rica to the Island, bringing them mail and further supplies. In addition, she was to bring the three deserters' wives back to the mainland, so that they could join their husbands and thereafter return to Germany with them.[68]

Clearly, the colony was not going well; but it may have served Gissler's purpose well enough, because one of the key ideas in his mind was to dig tunnels, in order to explore the possibility that the treasure was buried behind a rockfall. Every traveller to the Island in the years since 1908, when Gissler left, has commented on the complex system of tunnels which he dug out and constructed. It is inconceivable that he did all this by himself.

In 1897 Gissler became a Costa Rican citizen and was appointed Governor of the Island 'for so long as he remained there carrying out his work of coloniser and hunter of treasures'.[69] Why?

It is noticeable that the appointment came hard on the heels of the visit paid to the Island by the British warship, *H.M.S. Impérieuse*. As we know, her master, Captain Palliser had a private interest in the treasure and, being far from home, could more or less do as he liked, although he was officially on duty. He sent several platoons of marines ashore, with shovels and picks and large quantities of dynamite; and they dug and blasted several huge holes, telling Mrs. Gissler to mind her own business, when she protested. Gissler (who was away at the time) recorded this comment later:

---

68 D-L, 152-7
69 H& W, 123, C.Weston, 108.

> For the sake of the British Navy, I hate to believe that Palliser acted under instructions from his government, but if greed of money can lead a British admiral so far to forget himself as to violate private rights, what can be expected from the rough sailors who carried out his orders?[70]

It was not just the Royal Navy whom the Costa Ricans had to fear. There is some evidence (admittedly slender) of official German interest in the Island as early as 1884, and there was still the possibility of a descent on the Island by American filibusters. In the *New York Times* interview Gissler explained that:

> When a filibustering expedition came to Cocos from San Francisco – you read about it, of course - they landed and told me they had come to search the island and intended to kill all the game on it. I called the captain of the ship into my room and, showing him my credentials as Governor, told him that if he dared touch a piece of my property I would regard him as a pirate and treat him and his crew as such. I showed him the flag of Costa Rica flying above our heads and said he would be called to account for any violation of my rights. He was no fool, that fellow. I had my pistols on at the time, ready to use them. He had the good sense to apologize and sail away with his crew of adventurers.[71]

In appointing Gissler as Governor, the Costa Ricans were not merely bolstering his position, they were supporting their own claim to sovereignty. However, in this case, the Costa Ricans were also appointing a man with a proven record of being able to stand up for himself. In that same interview of 1907, Gissler gave an account of a rebellion amongst the Germman colonists, which he had crushed single-handedly.

---

70 H&W, 122.
71 H&W, 306.

"I took out eighteen Germans once, with their families, and thought they would raise great crops and all get rich, but in a short time they raised an insurrection instead."

"What became of the insurrection?"

"I quelled it."

"Tell me how?"

"I declared martial law, as Governor of the island, and with my big pistols pointed in the faces of the Germans scared them into submission. They laid down what arms they had and peace was restored. But the incident induced me to ship the whole caboodle away."

"You are Governor, General, Colonel, and the whole army, as well as lord high executioner, judge, jury, and undertaker?"

"Everything, I suppose.[72]

Despite Gissler's resilience, his colony failed soon afterwards. A photo taken in 1897 shows him on a beach with a dog and only six other colonists; but it seems that even the last of these left the Island in 1898. When Hervey de Montmorency landed in 1903 he found the German alone with his wife and one servant.[73]

This did not put an end to Gissler's treasure-hunting acitivties; and, although he did not live on the Island continuously, he does seem to have performed a useful role for Costa Rica, in policing the Island. On the other hand, it appears that the Costa Ricans wanted to have their cake and eat it, in the sense that they still wanted to be able to grant concessions to explore and excavate, and did not want to be prevented from doing this by their Governor, if the terms were right.

Thus in 1901, a new treasure-hunting company was formed in Vancouver, with a capital of $10,000, Gissler got wind of the project and recorded his objection:

---

72 Hancok & Weston, 306.
73 K, 23; C.Weston, 123; Montmorency, 230.

Allow me to inform you that no company with any such intent would have the right to land on Cocos Island, as I hold a concession from the authorities in regard to the said treasure, in which concession the Costa Rica government has an interest. Certainly anything that might be undertaken from Vancouver would amount to naught without my consent.

In the second half of 1901, Gissler went to the U.S.A. for over a year, leaving his wife alone on Cocos, and returning only in December 1902. Yet, when Hervey de Montmorency landed in 1903 he found that the Gisslers had constructed a comfortable house and seemed largely self-sufficient. They grew bananas, oranges, limes, vines, pines, potatoes, yams, maize and other fruits and vegetables, as well as coffee; Gissler made cigars from his own tobacco, rope from banana fibre, while the tannic acid he made from the bark of a tulip tree was used to make ink and tan the hides of wild pigs.[74]

Montmorency thought Gissler 'a man of resource and invention', a modern Robinson Crusoe, who had suffered much at the hands of other explorers. Accordingly he had good reason to be wary of strangers. Nevertheless he welcomed Montmorency and his party and was remarkably open about the great project of his life. Likewise, he behaved impeccably towards Fitzwilliam and his party at the beginning of 1905. He asked the Earl who he was, where he had come from, and what he wanted, though he also told him that, if he had come in search of treasure, he could not help him, as there was another party who already had a valid and exclusive concession. (By this, he meant Harold S. Gray's party). However, when Fitzwilliam replied that he had travelled to San José to obtain clarification of his own concession from the Costa Rican President, Gissler changed his tune. He became amicable, and he and Fitzwilliam had a long conversation in private. However, this did not stop him from entering into partnership with Gray, when he arrived on board the *Rose Marine* in February 1905, just after Fitzwilliam had left.[75]

---

74 C.Weston, 127; *Dundee Evening Post*, 12 January 1905.
75 C.Weston, 127; E.F.T.I., 21, 28-9, 115-116 (Guido).

COCOS ISLAND AND THE TREASURE OF LIMA

Whereas other travellers say that Gissler lived alone, or alone with his wife (and possibly a servant) for much of the time, an incident related in Agustin Guido's account of a Costa Rican visit to Gissler's camp in 1905 tells us that, for a while, there was a garrison of a dozen soldiers on the Island. Guido also tells us how Gissler related how the treasure had been brought to the Island in the first place. This is very intriguing, since his theories had clearly changed a good deal since his original encounter with Manoel Cabral in the 1880s. The German now thought that, although his own searches had been unsuccessful, there were three deposits of treasure on the Island, and one of them had been partially discovered by John Keating of Newfoundland, in 1846. Was this the Treasure of Lima? Presumably, it was; but Gissler did not use that name, nor did he refer to Captain Thompson or the *Mary Dear*, when explaining Keating's history.[76]

After Gissler finally left the Island, he admitted that he had only ever found 33 gold pieces, minted between 1773 and 1799, and a gold gauntlet. Some think that the fact that he found so many coins of 18th century date, indicates that he must also have found a larger hoard or hoards, from which these emanated; but this does not necessarily follow, and Christopher Weston has pointed out that the coins could well have been dropped by a member of one of the many hundreds of ships' crews which stopped off at the Island during the 19th century, whilst on legitimate business.[77]

Gissler died in New York in 1935, at the age of 78. His spirit was not broken. At the end of his life, he could still write:

> The treasure is on the island, but it will take money and a good deal of effort to unearth it. I have gone through many hardships and dangers and perhaps shall have to do so again, but this will not keep me away.

Gissler also made a will, in which he bequeathed half Cocos Island to various relatives and friends, estimating its value at not less than $200,000, though

---

76 C.Weston, 112-116.
77 Weston appears in *Jäger verlorener Schätze - Die Schatzinsel* (DMZ 2001).

for probate purposes his estate was valued at a mere $500. Some of his heirs even wrote to the Costa Rican government to ask about the value of their inheritance and inquire when they could take possession. The answer given was 'nothing', since Gissler was merely Governor of the island, not its owner, whatever he may have thought.

The difference of opinion is hardly surprising. Gissler had never fallen out with the Costa Ricans, and his relations with Presient Yglesias (1894-1902) seem to have been particularly friendly; but that does not mean that the government always saw eye to eye with the German. Gissler thought he had been appointed Governor, but also that he had property rights in the Island, by virtue of a certificate purporting to be issued by the Consul-General of Costa Rica to the U.S.A. in New York on December 14 1905. This stated that he:

> According to a contract made with the Government of Costa Rica in the year 1894 is the owner of half of the territory of the Island and has the right to exploit the other half in accordance with the stipulations of the above mentioned contract.[78]

If this document is genuine, it seems to refer to the new deal agreed between Gisser and Yglesias in 1895, rather than 1894; but in any event, Gissler misunderstood the Costa Rican position. They surely had no interest in maintaining his position on the Island once he and his colonists had gone; and as Gissler himself lived in the U.S.A. between 1908 and 1935.

Gissler has inspired a number of films, notably *Die Kokosinsel - Schatzinsel der Piraten* This features a panoply of historians, adventurers and experts; and they concentrate on Gissler, almost to the exclusion of everything else. His search may have been in vain; but the film-makers clearly view his failure as heroic. They point out that whilst some treasure-seekers lasted only a few days on the Island, Gissler lasted eighteen years.

---

78 C.Weston, 130-1 (where a copy of the certificate is reproduced).

In the 1960s Fritz Fischer re-wrote the history of the First World War in terms of Germany's 'Grab for World Power' (*Griff nach der Weltmacht*); but in fact, the new German Empire created in 1871 had started to flex her muscles in the 1890s. By then she had acquired an industrial and economic strength equal (if not superior) to Britain's and she wanted a Navy and colonies to match. She had duly acquired some territories, in Africa and New Guinea; but she had no colonies in the Americas, partly no doubt because of the Monroe Doctrine of 1823, which held that further efforts by European nations to take control of any independent state in North or South America would be regarded as 'the manifestation of an unfriendly disposition toward the United States.'

When interviewed in 1907, Gissler told the *New York Times* that, in his view, France and Great Britain each had designs on Cocos Island, saying in particular that 'England cannot afford to lose the opportunity to get Cocos Island' and again that 'England wants to obtain possession of Cocos Island for a coaling station.' The reporter asked whether British interference there would not be regarded as incompatible with the Monroe Doctrine; but Gissler did not think so.

> I do not think [the Monroe Doctrine] would be operative in the case of Cocos Island, but I may be mistaken. I do not think the Monroe Doctrine would cover an island over 300 miles from the mainland and in the Pacific Ocean.

The question remains as to whether Gissler's occupation of Cocos Island, and his establishment of a small German colony there, was part of Kaiser Wilhem II's imperial and colonial policy. The answer is, probably not. Gissler does not seem to have had any official contact with Berlin; and, although his colonists were undoubtedly of German stock, they were brought to the Island by agreement with the government of Costa Rica. Moreover, he lived for a time in Hawaii, his early business contacts were in the United States, and the principal document on which he relied to give him title to Cocos Island was drawn up in English and in New York, where he lived in later life. He told the American reporter in 1907, 'I cannot sell… without the consent of my government', by which he meant the Costa Rican.[79] The conclusion must be that he was very much his own man, not the Kaiser's.

What of the suggestion that Britain and France coveted the Island as a coaling station? This may well have been more than a figment of Gissler's imagination. In the 1890s, the world's steamships ships used coal rather than oil, and the British must have felt at least some concern that they had no coaling station of their own between the Falkland Islands in the South Atlantic and Esquimalt in Canada. Cocos Island was volcanic in origin and much too young, geologically speaking, to have economic deposits of coal; but, as Gissler said, coal could have been brought in from Australia; and Gissler's extensive tunnels could have provided the foundations for a series of bunkers. The idea was not so wild then, as it may appear to be now.

---

79 C. Weston, 131;H&W, 307.

Chapter 6

THE FOREIGN OFFICE

> "The revolution which brought modern science, technology and economy… made Europe into the centre of the world and a few European states into the lords of the globe."
>
> ERIC HOBSBAWM, *ON HISTORY* (1997)

There is a file in the National Archives at Kew which is described as an 'Enquiry regarding the Cocos Island treasure, Code 405 file 191.'[80] It was generated in 1949, because a certain Mr Dyson had written from the North of England to the Ministry of Foreign Affairs in Costa Rica, asking to be put in touch with the brothers Charles and James Forbes, 'who are attempting another search for the treasure of 15,000,000 [pounds?] believed buried in the Cocos Islands [sic] in the Pacific.' Although Dyson was said or thought to be a journalist, his letter was not grammatically written and he got the name of the Island wrong. Nevertheless, the Costa Ricans had forwarded his enquiry to the Foreign Office.

---

80 TNA FO 370/1838. There is also another file, FO 371/17/422, which relates to a similar request for information made on 21/12/1906 and a note: 'Cox to give advice and unspecified assistance to Mr Thomas Robinson of Streatham who proposes to search for treasure on Cocos Island.' I was not able to inspect this.

The reply, sent on behalf of the Foreign Secretary Ernest Bevin on 18 May 1949, said little: the Foreign Office had no knowledge of Forbes's proposed search, and the enquirer should refer back to the Costa Rican government, who should know more, since they had the power to grant concessions. The civil service had wanted to be of more assistance. A senior officer had suggested that Dyson also be referred to Peace Handbook no 141-2, entitled *Malpelo, Cocos and Easter Islands*, which had been published by Her Majesty's Stationery Office in 1920. However, a junior civil servant found that there were no copies available, and so the unelpful reply was sent.

Peace Handbook 141-2 can easily be purchased now. It had started life as one of a large number of studies commissioned from professional historians at the behest of the Foreign Office, for British delegates at the Versailles Peace Conference of 1919. Moreover, although it undoubtedly contains some errors, the Handbook was based on thorough research and was clearly and concisely written; but why, we may ask, was it written at all? Why did the British delegates to the Versailles Peace Conference need briefing about three small islands in remote regions of the Pacific, when the countries with the best claims to them (Colombia, Costa Rica and Chile) were not important combatants in the First World War?

The answer so far as Cocos Island is concerned may have something to do with the political situation in Costa Rica, because in January 1917, General Federico Tinoco Granados (1868 – 1931) had seized power in a coup d'état and established a military dictatorship. Though his government declared war on Germany in May 1918, it failed to win recognition from the United States, and as a result Costa Rica was not even represented at Versailles.

There may have been another reason too. The British may simply have wanted their diplomats to be armed with information of all kinds, from all around the globe. Britain was still a world-power, and one of the countries which had done most to defeat Imperial Germany; and the British doubtless expected to have significant influence in the re-drawing of boundaries after the War, and in the re-allocation of Germany's overseas possessions. Accordingly, it seems as if they wanted to know in detail whether there were any territories in the world which were still unclaimed, given the possibilities, one imagines, for swaps and trade-offs with the Americans, French and Japanese, all of which had also been on the winning side, as well as having Empires, formal or informal, in and around the Pacific Ocean.

In addition to sections on the position and extent, surface and coast, climate, sanitary conditions, and population of Cocos Island, the Peace Handbook deals with 'Products'.

> Luxuriant tropical forest covers practically the whole island. There are many kinds of hard timber trees, such as are found in Central America, and two species of palms. The coconut palm, the prevalence of which gave the island its name, is now rare and scarcely found, except in the interior, but it certainly could be replanted. There are many tree-ferns. Besides timber trees there are a few plants of economic value, such as the guava, pawpaw, lemon, and pumpkin. Most of these have probably been introduced by settlers at one time or another.
>
> Except for the difficulty of finding level land and keeping down the forest growth, most tropical crops might be cultivated. Certainly a considerable amount of fruit could be grown.
>
> There is little animal life. Wild pigs, descendants of those left by Colnett in 1793, thrive, and rats, also introduced, are numerous. There is one species of snake and a lizard. In the coastal waters there are turtle. Sea-birds are numerous, and there are a few land species, including ducks. In the surrounding seas there are plenty of good edible fish.

The somewhat inaccurate section in the Handbook on 'Ownership' suggests that, in the British view, the Costa Rican claim to Cocos Island was not unimpeachable.

> With regard to the nationality of Cocos Island no clear statement has been met with dating earlier than 1888, in which year, according to

Mr. de Montmorency, the German (or, according to *The Times* supplement, Swiss) settler Gieseler, or Geisler, was granted a concession in the island by the Costa Rican Government, with a nomination as governor, a post which had never previously been created there, as the island was uninhabited. Gieseler, who with his wife and'one native labourer from the continent then formed the entire population of the island, finally quitted it in the steamer *Lytton* (late *Scotia*) with the Montmorency expedition in 1903; and in 1911 he was living at Punta Arenas (Costa Rica).

It was Gieseler's homestead that was seen in 1897 in Wafer Bay, and reported by the officer commanding H.M.S. *Icarus*, Comdr. E. J. Fleet, as 'a small settlement of four or five huts, where the Costa Rica colours were flying'.

An examination of Don Manuel M. de Peralta's *Aperçu critique*, submitted to the President of the French Republic as arbitrator on the boundary question between Costa Rica and Colombia in 1900, reveals no mention whatever of Cocos Island, nor of any Costa Rican territorial claim to seaward of Cocos Island.

The Handbook also provides some evidence that the French had designs on the Island; and France was, of course, the host of the Versailles Peace Conference, as well as being one of the main victims of German aggression, for which she sought reparations, on a large scale. The only surprising thing is that little Cocos Island should have been thought to be in the frame, when these great questions of diplomacy were being discussed.

> In the excellent descriptive account by Assistant Paymaster D. Lièvre, of the French navy, this officer ignores the existence of any sovereign rights over it and discusses the possible advantages France might derive by taking possession of it. Lièvre's articles were published in 1893. Incidentally, he mentions that Clipperton Island, the nearest land to Cocos Island on the west-north-west, did at that time belong to France.

COCOS ISLAND AND THE TREASURE OF LIMA

The Foreign Office's conclusions on the diplomatic question were contained in a final section entitled 'General Observations'. Perhaps surprisingly, in view of the fact that France was our principal ally and friend in Europe, the F.O. did not back the French claim, but it did leave the question of ownership open to some doubt.

> In so far as its known history points, the administration of Cocos Island by the Government of Costa Rica dates from 1888. Prior to the year 1821 the State of Costa Rica was a Spanish possession from the beginning of the sixteenth century. At that time, and for 300 years afterwards, the Spanish monarchs and people believed in the temporal efficacy of the Papal Bull of Alexander VI, as amended by the Treaty of Tordesillas in 1494, and claimed sovereign rights over all the islands to the westward of the American continent, as far as a meridian passing through the East Indies. It was on this basis that Viceroys of Peru despatched expeditions of discovery into the Pacific Ocean, of which Mendafia's to the Solomon Islands, Queiros's in search of a southern continent, Gonzalez's to Easter Island, and Boenechea's to Tahiti (places much more remote from the continent than Cocos Island is) afford examples.
>
> Hence, when in 1821 Costa Rica declared itself independent of the mother country, its rulers would, in the ordinary course, view Cocos Island, which is only 260 miles distant, as an appurtenance, if not an integral part, of the *terrain* of the new republic. Geographically considered such a claim must be conceded; and there is little doubt that popular opinion and national sentiment in Costa Rica would oppose any suggestion to the contrary. Moreover, some thirty years have passed, without challenge, since the Ministry appointed Gieseler their governor in the island; and it is a principle of international law that *Qui prior est tempore potior est jure*.[81] In other words, Costa Rica is daily acquiring a prescriptive ownership by priority of occupation.

---

81 The earlier claim is the stronger in law.

This passage provides some support for the Costa Rican claim to Cocos Island, rather than the French; but at the same time it refers to a prescriptive claim only, and 'prescription' is not the only basis for claiming the ownership of territory in international law. It is not as strong, for example, as 'cession' or 'effective occupation.'

However, the main point to be made here is that, even in this legalistic account of diplomatic history, there was no getting away from the fabulous treasure.

> It was stated by the late Colonel Church, in an article contributed by him to the *Geographical Journal* in 1897, that there were ten colonists (at Cocos Island) in 1894, part of the emigrants sent there under a contract with the Costa Rica Government to establish an agricultural colony. It was, however, suspected that the real object of the *empresario* was to hunt for immense treasures in gold bars said to have been buried in three separate parcels in as many localities by the pirate Benito; or, according to another story, by the captain of an English brig, to whom the treasure was entrusted in Peru during the War of Independence.

The Peace Handbook also contains a Chronological Summary, which states that from 1873 onwards, there were 'various unsuccessful attempts to find the concealed treasure', although, as we have seen there were more than a few expeditions before that. The following paragraph is of greater interest:

> In 1818 or 1819 a notorious pirate known as Benito, *alias* Bennett Graham, [hid] a vast plunder he had obtained by rifling certain churches in Peru. A few years afterwards, it is said, Benito deposited a fresh quantity of gold bars and specie, worth eleven million dollars. In or about 1826 a man passing as William Thompson, who appears to have previously served under Benito, but was then in command of the brig *Mary Read,* concealed about twelve million dollars' worth of stolen gold coin, jewels, and silver ingots on Cocos Island.

This is a curious account, considering that it emanated from an official source. First the writers have heard of Thompson (or at least of a man 'passing as Thompson'), and of his ship, but they got the name of the ship wrong, as well as the date of Thompson's raid on Callao. Did they mean to say 1821, rather than 1826? If so, it is curious that they do not mention any Viceroy or indeed the Peruvian Revolution; but perhaps they did mean 1826, and took this date from Ricardo Palma's *Dos Milliones*, a fictional account of a piratical 'affair' which took place that year, which bears some resemblance to the story of Captain Thompson, though there are also numerous differences. In any event, they do not cite any of the numerous contemporary British witnesses whose accounts must have been available to them (see Chapter 9).

As for the sources they did use, the authors of the Handbook say:

> Some of the circumstances of the three lodgements of treasure at the island, and of efforts that have been made for its recovery, are related (by persons who were more or less concerned in the matter) in documents preserved at the Admiralty.

Now this is surprisingly vague. Most professional historians, working in the first decades of the 20th century, belonged to the school of Leopold von Ranke and Lord Acton. These people believed in the prime importance of documents, rather than memoirs or narratives; and one would therefore have expected that these Admiralty documents would have been cited. They are not; and the reason appears to be that they could not be cited, because they did not exist. Certainly no other historian has ever discovered any documentary confirmation of what is supposed to have happened in Peru 1818, or 1819, or 1826, or for that matter 1821, so far as the treasures of Cocos Island are concerned. But the Handbook continues, in a remarkably frank vein.

> An attempt to piece the facts together in the form of a narrative is embodied in a book called *On the Track of a Treasure,* by Mr. Hervey de

Montmorency. Another book, by Mr. Ralph D. Paine, contains a chapter on the subject under the heading 'The Lure of Cocos Island', much of which is culled from the former book. Both these books are of the sketchy or 'popular' order, and the narratives they present cannot be accepted without reserve. Certain names of persons, and of at least one ship, have also been transfigured; but anyone with knowledge of the facts will find little difficulty in recognizing the pseudonyms adopted.

The authors of the Handbook have rather given the game away here: they say they have relied heavily on Montmorency and Paine, while admitting the severe limitations of both these works. And, with hindsight, we can see that the following paragraph discredits the Foreign Office view still further,

> A treasure search expedition was organized by a syndicate formed by Lord Fitzwilliam, under a concession held by Mr. Gissler (or Gieseler), who lived on the island for many years. At the same time the Costa Rican Government granted a similar concession to a Mr. T. Robinson. The Costa Rican Government professed, at first, to regard Lord FitzWilliam's expedition as a filibustering one; but ultimately the Fitzwilliam and Robinson parties came to an agreement and joined forces in an attempt to discover the treasure, which was not successful.

Thanks to the re-discovery of George Eustace Cooke-Yarborough's account of Earl Fitzwilliam's voyage of 1904-5, we now know that the above account is highly inaccurate. In particular, Fitzwiliam obtained no concession from Gissler; and there was no joining of forces between Fitzwilliam and Robinson, or anyone else.

Notwithstanding these errors, the Handbook stated its conclusions on this point very confidently; and these were to be repeated over and over in years to come.

Not less than a dozen organized attempts to recover the buried treasure have been made. Clues to the spot where one batch of treasure was deposited have led some of the searchers to a marked rock; and one man is said to have come upon some gold bars and kegs of Spanish coin through an accidental fall over the face of a scarp. A silver ecclesiastical cross was also found in the bed of a stream. But the main stores of treasure are still hidden, in spite of various excavations and blasting operations which have been undertaken from time to time...

The existence of treasure concealed in the island is well established, and has been a matter of notoriety among residents not only of Costa Rica but of all the principal coast towns from Lima to Vancouver for many years.[82]

The adventurer, and the investor, intending to try his luck would not be put off by reading the Handbook published in 1920. Moreover, since the publication was official, and we know that civil servants routinely issued it to anyone who enquired about Cocos Island, it would undoubtedly have come to the attention of a wide section of the public.

By casting doubt on the Costa Rican claim to sovereignty over Cocos Island, and by suggesting that there was indeed buried treasure to be found there, the Foreign Office helped to revive the myth, which had been subjected to ridicule in many newspapers prior to 1914. From this moment on promoters of all kinds could point to an official British view which supported their schemes. In 1934, when Commander Worsley, of Treasure Recovery Ltd., was asked to explain why the company had not sought permission from Costa Rica to land on the Island, he explained

That the misunderstanding arose from a belief that it was doubtful if any nation could establish ownership of the Island.[83]

---

82 H.M.S.O., 20,25.
83 *The Times*, 16 October 1934.

In 1922, treasure-hunting received another considerable fillip, when Howard Carter discovered the fabulous tomb of Tutankhamun in the Valley of the Kings in Egypt. It may seem odd that this should have stimulated a renewed interest in the Treasure of Lima; but, to the adventurer, Carter's discovery demonstrated that, if one persevered long enough, rejecting the criticism of the doubting Thomases, one could hope to succeed in the end. Carter had repeatedly been told that he was engaged in a fool's errand, but he eventually astonished everyone, when he succeeded in finding those 'wonderful things', after fifteen years of patient archaeology; and his excavation of the tomb continued to enthrall the civilised world all through the 1920s. Indeed 'King Tut' has continued to fascinate us ever since. The Costa Rican historian, Raul Arias, for one, has drawn a parallel between Carter's search and the search for the Treasure of Lima. The message is clear – don't give up, keep looking.

Chapter 7

THE BOOM YEARS

When Earl Fitzwilliam made the journey to Cocos Island in 1904, he had the benefit of technology which was greatly superior technology to that available to the mythical Captain Thompson, or the real Admiral Cochrane, in 1821. He went on board a steamship, burning coal in large quantities. While in transit, he sent messages by telegram, making use of transoceanic cables which spanned the globe. He took a team of miners, mining engineers and a doctor; and while he was on the Island, at least one of his team took photographs.

After the First World War, adventurers could use the Panama Canal; and in the main they now went in oil-fired ships. In addition to dynamite and gelignite, they had radio, metal detectors and excavating machines. Much later, they were able to make use of low-flying aircraft, helicopters and satellites. But the spirit of adventure being what it is, not all of them chose to avail themselves of these opportunities. Some preferred to do things in the old-fashioned way, going with a skeleton crew on board sailing ships, and employing traditional diviners.

Before 1914, many of the British who went to Cocos Island were rich enough to pay for their expeditions themselves, or obtained the funds from wealthy friends and sponsors. Palliser was a high ranking officer in the Royal

Navy, Montmorency an army officer, Fitzwilliam a major landowner and coal magnate, while Davis and Till were 'society ladies'. These people went in search of adventure as well as treasure, though Fitzwilliam always claimed he went in search of coal and minerals, and the ladies said their motives were philanthropic. In the United States, the adventurers came from the business class; and they often used limited companies to raise capital. After 1918, the way lay open to a wider class of adventurer; and, though we still see voyages undertaken by American tycoons, we also find plainer and poorer men taking part in the game, the classic case being Commander Plumpton of Cullompton, in Devon.

The 'boom' in treasure-hunting in the 1930s was remarked upon in the magazine *Britannia and Eve* on 1 October 1938. The article listed dozens of searches, for lost treasures of all kinds, all around the world, though in particular in Latin America; but the author was clearly a sceptic.

> Searching for lost treasure is indeed becoming rationalised – one of the minor but more adventurous industries of our money-obsessed world. There are joint-stock companies whose business is treasure-hunting. One with a capital of £50,000 is called 'Treasure Recovery Ltd.' During the last ten months I have thrice been shown in confidence old stained charts by men desirous of finding backers for a new quest for some ancient golden fleece; and I have been five times invited to participate financially in organised searches for treasure which, if located and recovered, would amount in the aggregate to £37,000,000…
>
> On my desk (it reached many other desks!) lies an invitation to risk money in a search for the treasure of the Incas. "Millions of pounds" worth of gold lie buried in that part of South America which was once the Empire of the Incas," says the prospectus. Yes, and there is also coal under the polar ice, and a needle in a haystack somewhere in England.
>
> Total cost of Cocos quests to date, probably half a million. Total recoveries, a spade and a doubloon.

BRITISH EXPEDITIONS

Space allows us to look at only a few of the expeditions undertaken from British shores in the years between the two World Wars.

SIR MALCOLM CAMPBELL, 1926

In 1926 Sir Malcolm Campbell (1885 – 1948) took up the baton. People of my generation remember his son Donald, who was killed when his boat *Blue Bird* turned over on Coniston Water in the Lake District in 1967; but the father was more famous than the son in his day, setting no less than 13 land and water speed world records.

Sir Malcolm travelled to Cocos Island with Lee Guinness (1887 – 1937), a member of the Irish brewing family who once held the world land speed record himself, and invented the spark plug. Guinness provided the yacht, suitably called *Adventuress*; and they used used the Panama Canal. Campbell describes its technological marvels in Chapter VIII of his book, *My Greatest Adventure* (1932); and it clearly shortened his journey considerably.

On the other hand, developments in technology do not seem to have assisted him greatly in any other way. There is no reference in his book to radio; and, so far as detection of treasure was concerned, he thought it would be hopeless to rely on a human metal diviner but, after many frustrating experiments with electrical instruments, he concluded that these were of no use either.[84] As a result, he seems to have been entirely reliant, once he reached the Island, on having an accurate 'clue', which told him the supposed whereabouts of a treasure-cave.

When he was unable to find the cave, Sir Malcolm tried blasting a rock, which he thought might be hiding the entrance. He describes this in Chapter XI, using language which was typical of his class and his age:

> We drilled holes all around [the rock], plugged them with dynamite and blew great chunks out until we had completely blasted the top away. There were no traces of a cave, and the rock, like the nigger's

---

84 Campbell, 67-72.

head, seemed to be solid right through. We blasted several other large boulders in the immediate neighbourhood and finally came to the conclusion that it was a waste of time and dynamite to hunt round any further in that locality. [85]

Campbell summarised his experience in a letter dated 29 April 1930.

I visited Cocos Island in 1926 with a small party of friends who were not really enthusiastic over this treasure hunt, they all being too sceptical and believed that the whole thing was a fairy story. My friends expected that they would come across the treasure five minutes after landing and, because we were not immediately successful, they lost heart. I lived on the island with two seamen in a tent for a matter of seventeen days.[86]

A second Campbell-Guinness expedition was planned for 1931; but a reporter for the *Hartlepool Mail* thought that the voyage was something of a joke.

It is a pity there is no golf-course on Cocos Island. I do not think they will find much else to do there. The last time I was in Panama, a Cuban showed me a map of Cocos Island. He pointed to a cross on the map at the foot of a hill.

"Under that spot, Señor" he said impressively "Is buried gold, silver, and jewels worth £6,000,000".

"Why hasn't anyone got it out?" I asked.

"They didn't have the equipment" he said.

Since then I have heard all over South America of the treasure of Cocos, which has been valued at £2,000,000, £4,000,000, £5,000,000 and £8,000,000. I have seen three other maps of the

---

85 Campbell, 223.
86 *The Observer*, 12 January 2003; Hancock & Weston, 129, 141.

island. Scores of people have dug it up until it looked like a rabbit warren but all the treasure seems still to be there. It is now valued, I read last night, at £12,000,000. But they will have to hurry. For three weeks ago I met a man who was on the eve of sailing for the Island himself. He thinks there is only £8,000,000 there. If he gets there first, I hope there won't be a fight over all this wealth.'[87]

The second expedition never materialised, but Campbell now wrote about his first. He was clearly a man of action; but what sort of historian was he? Initially he did at least consider the evidence. His first chapter is entitled 'Buried Treasure' and he tells us about the legends attaching to various hoards around the world, remarking that

> There is hardly a port in the world that does not contain its tarry-breeked, rum-smelling, tale-pitching crop of liars ready to whisper you tales and sell you charts, to urge you to up-sail and away. You will find them from Plymouth to Penang, from Vancouver to Vladivostok, from London to Long Island.

Campbell eventually decided that Cocos Island was a better bet than any other place in the world. He studied the history of the Island, and found that there were three possible treasures which might await discovery

> The first is that of Captain Edward Davis, a partner with Dampier in his privateering adventures, when he blockaded the Bay of Panama and sacked the City of Leon in Nicaragua in 1685. The second is that of Benito Bonito, "Bonito of the Bloody Sword," a pirate of the early eighteen hundreds, and the third is the famous treasure of the City of Lima, which was buried on Cocos in about 1821, by a Captain Thompson, a Scotch merchant skipper, who turned pirate and joined Bonito on the high seas.

---

87   *Hartlepool Mail*, 20 November 1931.

Finally, Campbell decided that the third, the so-called Treasure of Lima, was potentially the greatest prize of the three. However, he was labouring under several misapprehensions. For example, he thought that Lima was liberated by Simon Bolivar in 1821, when it was actually José de San Martin who marched into the city. He also thought that the Royalist in office at the time was a mere Governor, when he would have been one of two Viceroys. Lastly, he appears to have thought that Captain Thompson was a Scot, while also being an Anglo-Saxon who (of course) had a reputation for fair dealing and honesty; and, when he lands in Wafer Bay, he mistakes August Gissler's camp for Earl Fitzwilliam's, when the latter never camped there.[88]

This is not the worst of it, because Campbell routinely engaged in flights of fancy, for which he made no apology. So, he simply invented a scene where the fabled Treasure was taken away by Thompson and his crew.

> We may imagine the scene under the torrid blue skies of that South American day, with the spire of the great cathedral upthrust above the roofs of the white houses and the narrow streets alive with anxious, jostling crowds. Then, forcing a passage through them, a long line of packladen mules, carrying bullion from the banks, solid bars of gold, the jewels and plate of the chief inhabitants, and finally, in two great wooden boxes, the golden Virgin and Child from the cathedral.

There is much more of this stuff. Instead of citing primary sources, Sir Malcolm simply adopted them as fact, mixed them up, and embroidered them. This is permissible in a novelist, but not in a historian; and, in the end it is clear that Campbell did not go on the expedition because he examined the evidence for the existence of the Treasure of Lima and found it convincing. He simply had a blind faith in its existence, just as he believed that there were Inca survivors living in the interior of Cocos Island; and he retained this faith, even after he returned to England empty-handed.

---

88 Campbell, 44, 46 & 172.

> I am still certain that [the Treasure] lies somewhere near the spot where we found the jumble of rocks and blasted the top off the great rock that had three cracks in it.

Campbell's book does however throw light on one of the routes by which the traditional story has come down to us. He tells us that he finally decided to embark for Cocos Island when he had lunch with Commodore Curzon-Howe, son of Admiral Sir Assheton Gore Curzon-Howe (1850-1911), who had received a letter from Nicholas Fitzgerald, revealing his secret (see Appendix).

In 1932 Campbell, who was by now world-famous as a sportsman, despite the failure of his first expedition to Cocos Island, set up a company with the aid of a Colonel Leckie, in order to finance further attempts to find the treasure. This was Cocos Island Treasure Ltd., and it issued a prospectus featuring a galleon on the cover, referring to Colonel Leckie's new metal detecting device, the 'Metalaphone', as a crucial tool in the company's possession, and promising investors a return of $600 for every $2 they were willing to contribute. The prospectus also contained a further promise.

> The treasure hunt will give you all the thrills and excitement of the sweepstake, the horse race, the lottery, with the added satisfaction,
>
> *IF ANYONE WINS, - EVERYONE WINS*

The expedition never even left Vancouver. The last promise did, however come to the attention of an investor who would prove to be Campbell's nemesis – Admiral Chambers. His devastating critique of the search for the Treasure of Lima was published only three years later.

COMMANDER PLUMPTON, 1932

By 1931, the phrase 'Cocos Island treasure' had entered the language, albeit temporarily, as indicating a windfall which would rescue the unfortunate from money worries;[89] but some of those who went to the Island could have done with financial assistance even before they set off. Commander James Plumpton was one, for his expedition of 1932 operated on a shoe-string from start to finish.

A friend donated an ancient ketch-rigged trawler named *Vigilant*, which he had bought for a mere £250. The rest of the finance was raised by eight other friends or acquaintances, including Frank Cooper, who had a glove-making business in Yeovil. Plumpton contributed only £90 of his own money. Accordingly, although this expedition was made some thirty years after those undertaken by Palliser, Montmorency and Fitzwilliam, Plumpton did not derive many benefits from modern technology – he could not afford to. He had radios – both a 'Marconi set', and an 'Eddystone four valve' - but the *Vigilant* was a small wooden sailing ship built by Uphams of Brixton, and only 50 tons gross in weight, whereas Fitzwilliam's *Veronique* had been a steamship, 350 feet long, weighing 6,650 tons and capable of making over 300 miles a day.[90] This explains why Plumpton took four months to make the voyage from England to Cocos Island, despite passing through the Panama Canal, while Fitzwilliam made the considerably longer voyage through the Straits of Magellan in just over two.

Plumpton did his homework in relation to all things practical. Chapters I and II of his book are full of his dealings with the Admiralty and the Board of Trade (regarding insurance and so forth), the composition of the crew, and the purchase of supplies and equipment of all kinds. He refers in particular to 'a good medical outfit and a quantity of gelignite' – which demonstrates that, despite his reliance on sail rather than engine power, he was up to date in some areas.

---

89 *Dundee Courier*, 26 November 1931: "MAKE IT BOOKS THIS CHRISTMAS. PUBLISHERS have solved the problem of inexpensive Christmas presents. Books never come amiss, and the reading charm and material resplendency of this season's books are out of all proportion to modest costs. Bookmaking craft has bettered its best. Colour printing has created a new standard. Illustrators have worked in a morning mood of ardour. It would seem that in a world worried by money troubles some magic lamp has been rubbed, that some Cocos Island treasure has been discovered. Buying books for Christmas giftgiving becomes an exercise in thrift."
90 TNA, Transcript of Register for Transmission to Registrar-General of Shipping and Seamen, Form 19, *Véronique* (previously the *Harlech Castle*).

On the first page of his book, Plumpton openly tells us that, although the 'definite objective' of his voyage was to visit Cocos Island, he also hoped to call in at Grand Piton Island, and one of the Salvage Islands (in the Atlantic), where there was also supposed to be treasure.

He sailed via Madeira and the Canaries, St Vincent, and Trinidad. The voyage was uneventful, except that that they had some mechanical problems, and the boat suffered from Teredo worm, which meant that they had to scrape her bottom in Grand Piton Island. The crew seem to have remained cheerful, and there were some comical moments when they tried to make bread.

Like Fitzwilliam, Plumpton had to resort to subterfuge from time to time, to disguise the true nature of his voyage. When they met a 'murderous looking gang of Venezuelan fishermen' on the Testigo Islands, and were asked what they were doing there, the Brits replied that they were hoping to get a shipload of turtles, and take them back to Trinidad. However, when they met an American in Balboa, on the Pacific side of the Panama Canal, they told him of their quest. He then directed them to Montuoso and then to Cano Island (which belonged to Costa Rica, as Cocos did); and they landed on each in turn. They found Montuoso impossible to penetrate (and temporarily lost a man there) but spent two days digging on Cano, unearthing only pottery.[91]

When it came to finding treasure, Plumpton was initially dependant on the expertise of his companion Frank Cooper, who supposedly had an uncanny ability to detect precious metal with a spring extracted from an old gramophone;[92] but, once arrived on Cocos, he fell in with a party of Canadians who were engaged in the same search as he was, and had a 'Metalophone'; and Plumpton now describes this device.

> This was a long cable connected to a coil at each end, these coils being of either two, four or six feet in diameter, and constructed of a mass of fine wire wound in some intricate fashion. Electric current was passed

---
91 Plumpton, 66-67.
92 Plumpton 29, Chapter VI.

> through these coils, and it was alleged that sound would be given at the listening-end should these coils pass over hidden metal. The two-feet coils were reputed to act up to a depth of 25 feet and the six-feet ones up to 60 feet or more. Conclusive tests were said to have been carried out by the Metalophone Company, in which metal had been located on land at a depth of 50 feet and beneath water to a depth of over 100 feet.

The two parties agreed to join forces; but, in the event, the Metalophone did not work.

> It was a cumbersome affair to handle; the coils, cables and complete outfit weighing well over a hundredweight, and requiring four men to operate them. In that country, where there is practically no flat land, and tremendously thick undergrowth everywhere, it was difficult to use it satisfactorily. Failures were generally attributed to damp, and the coils repeatedly had to be baked, though it is hard to understand why this should have been so for the whole apparatus was heavily insulated and, one would have thought, entirely waterproof.[93]

Despite this tremendous setback, Plumpton did not think that the Metalophone was entirely without merit.

> It would be out of place to speak disparagingly of this instrument, for it is possible that, like many another amazing invention, it is still in its infancy, and still capable of being improved and developed until it will do what is claimed.

Plumpton did make another voyage, undaunted by his previous failure; and, once again, he took Frank Cooper of Yeovil with him. Their destination was kept secret, though the newspapers speculated that Plumpton's aim was to find a sunken Spanish galleon, full of gold bullion and silver cannons.

---

93 Plumpton 93-4.

This time, they ran out of luck rather more quickly: their ship *France* foundered in a storm some 33 miles off the coast of Guiana. Plumpton was found, after he had drifted for four days on the wreckage; but Frank Cooper never was.

Plumpton was an enterprising and resourceful man but he was a sailor, not a scholar. He clearly did some research (see Chapter V); and he formed the view that any treasure which might be found on Cocos Island must have been put there, not by Captain Thompson and the crew of the *Mary Dear* in 1821, but by the pirate Benito in 1818 or 1819. (Like others, he thought that this man might be one and the same as Captain Bennett Graham R.N.) On the other hand, when he found that the Canadians led by Colonel Leckie had a small boat named *Mary Dear*, he wrote:

> The boat was named *Mary Dear*, presumably after the famous brig which brought so it is said, at least one very big consignment of treasure to Cocos. The correct name of that ship, however, was *Mary Dier*, but probably the Canadians thought that 'Dear' sounded more homely.[94]

But can we trust Plumpton's research about historical matters when he jumps to the wrong conclusion, even about things he sees? When he arrives on the Island, he describes the remains of the huts in Wafer Bay, known by then as 'Pirate Village', as the remains of the penal colony established on the island by the Costa Ricans. In other words, he does not seem to have heard of August Gissler at all, though the German's long residence on the island was by now common knowledge. Plumpton also opines that previous expeditions had neglected the obvious fact that the treasure must have been hidden not very far from the high-water mark (because treasure is heavy, and the interior of Cocos Island is impenetrable); and he adds that 'the place is very likely further concealed by landslides, or falls of cliffs, which have since occurred.'[95] This is to ignore the fact that previous expeditions, such as Fitzwilliam's

---

94 Plumpton, 77-8, 85.
95 Plumpton, 177-8.

and Campbell's, had taken explosives, for the very purpose of blasting away landslides and supervening rocks.

WILKINS, 1932
Harold Tom Wilkins (1891—1960) was not an adventurer. He was a British journalist and prolific author. He wrote about a vanished white race which supposedly occupied the whole of South America in ancient times. He was also located the descendants of Atlantis in underground tunnels in South America, and was an advocate of U.F.Os; but *Treasure Hunting* (London (1932) is a different kind of work. Here, Wilkins is careful in his use of sources and sceptical of mere travellers' tales. He refers to 'the fevered brain' of some newspaper correspondents; and he is very ready to pick other writers up when they make elementary mistakes, such as when they confuse Cocos Island with the Cocos Keeling Islands, and when they describe it as being 'in the Spanish Main'. He quotes from Lord Cochrane, albeit selectively, but condemns Keating in round terms, for having left his wife a 'faked chart' when he died in 1882. He is almost rude about Campbell, despite the fact that the latter wrote a foreword to the book.[96]

Above all, Wilkins explains that there were commercial motives at work in the creation and growth of the myth of the Treasure of Lima. The way he puts this is to say that 'more gold came from Elstree and Holywood' than from piracy, in other words that many 20th century adventurers were more interested in the money to be made from film (and book) rights, than they were in finding buried treasure. He also points to the fact that the Costa Ricans long had an interest in promoting the myth, because they had the right to grant (and sell) concessions. He added that the terms of these concession were not always very clear – a problem which Fitzwilliam certainly encountered – but the resulting muddle presumably increased the profits derived from the business by the Costa Rican government.

---

96 Wilkins, 95, 99(n), 102(n).

Wilkins concludes by implying that the entire story of the Treasure of Lima and Cocos Island was a myth and perhaps also a hoax, from the very beginning.

"CAN you tell me where I can find a genuine treasure chart of Cocos Island? Where are the treasures cached on Cocos Island? If it's genuine, where can I obtain reliable information about it?" Hardly a month passes by in which I do not receive such inquiries in letters from men, women, youths, and even girls (!), in the U.S.A., in Canada, and right round the globe from Australia and New Zealand down under to countries on the European continent.

It is most singular that, in a presumably matter-of-fact, scientific age, such as that in which we are living, a little desert island, hardly more than six miles square, 550 miles S.W. of the Panama Canal, and a rendezvous of buccaneers and pirates since the days of Wafer, Davis, and Dampier, and probably of much earlier English and Spanish adventurers, should still draw like a powerful magnet men and women of so many different types.

There is an expedition at least once every year to this beckoning island, and countless must be the ships which, in the last sixty years or more, have come creeping back at night to moorings in 'Frisco Bay and the West India Dock, London, slipping into retired berths, and hoping no one will ask questions about the luck of their vain hunts.[97]

TREASURE RECOVERY LTD., 1934

Neither Montmorency, nor Earl Fitzwilliam, nor Campbell nor Plumpton ever found anything; but they all thought that it would be worthwhile to return to Cocos Island for a second try. And this was despite the fact that two of them met Gissler, and all knew of his long residence on the Island, and his strenuous efforts to find what they all sought for. None of them saw

---

97 Wilkins, 81.

through the myth, to the reality, which was that there was nothing there in the first place.

Some of them placed their hopes in modern science; and thought that if the right equipment was deployed, this would facilitate the search. This was certainly the view taken by the Canadians whom Plumpton encountered in 1932. The Metalophone had been developed by W.H.Clayton of the Canadian Clayton Metalophone Company, whose promoters included Colonel J.E. Leckie, Captain C.A. Arthur (whom we shall meet again) and Stratford Jolly (one of Plumpton's so-called 'friends.').[98] Clayton Metalophone seems to have ceased trading early in 1933; but in 1934, a new company was floated on the Stock Exchange.

This was Treasure Recovery Ltd., and its promoters included Rear-Admiral Lyne, Commander Worsley, Stratford Jolly, Commander Stenhouse, Captain Polkinghorne, and the inevitable Colonel Leckie, all of whom had extensive previous experience, either of the sea or of treasure-hunting. Polkinghorne claimed previous experience of Cocos Island itself, in 1925. Jolly claimed that he had been on the 'Spanish Main Treasure Expedition' of 1932-3.

The company was floated on the Stock Exchange, with the aim of raising £75,000 and of going in search of the 'numerous treasures' to be found on Cocos Island. The promoters responsible for the new company's prospectus felt obliged to describe the shares as 'definitely speculative'; but they were also able to say quite truthfully that the Peace Handbook (described in chapter 6 above) had stated that the existence of treasure on the island was 'well established'. They also made grand claims for the modernity of their methods.

> The methods to be employed on the expedition are strictly scientific, they having been subjected to many rigorous tests the field. The geo-electric and electro-magnetic methods which the company will employ in the search for Cocos Island treasures (in particular a patented property method (no 608/38 Patent Appd., Arthur Hale) are today extensively employed in important surveys.

---

98 Hancock & Weston, Chapter 15.

WHY METHODS HAVE NOT BEEN PREVIOUSLY EMPLOYED IN THE SEARCH FOR TREASURE – This is sufficiently explained by the fact that geo-electric methods are not generally known. They have been exclusively employed by Corporations interested in prospecting who are not concerned with any other operations. This expedition, owing to the specialized knowledge of the Directorate, will be the first to employ scientific methods of search.[99]

The promoters of the company were well-connected, and tried to exploit the strength of British snobbery. They pointed out that previous treasure-hunters had included Palliser and Montmorency in 1903, Fitzwilliam in 1904 and Campell in 1926 – which impliedly enlisted the support for the venture of one belted Earl, one knight of the realm, a senior army officer and a Royal Navy commander. They also held a lunch for their friends at the Travel Club in July 1934.[100]

The company prospectus promised that an expedition would be launched in April and would arrive on the Island in May.[101] In the event the new company mounted two expeditions. The first was undertaken on board the *Queen of Scots*, which (as *The Times* reported)[102] left England on 20 August 1934 and arrived in Wafer Bay on 26 September. The yacht was provided by a Mr Anthony Drexel junior, possibly the son of the American financier of the same name (1826-1893).

Before setting off, Captain Arthur again claimed that he would use the latest equipment: an aeroplane for surveying, electrical instruments for exploration, telephones for communication and the latest core-drills for digging.[103] The treasure awaiting discovery was now estimated to be worth between £12,000,000 and £25,000,000 and Arthur claimed that he knew exactly where it was; but he did not even bother to ask the Costa Ricans for permission to land. Instead, he laid claim to the Island in the name of the

---

99 *Western Morning News*, 17 March 1934. There is a copy of the prospectus in the British Library.
100 *The Times*, 31 July 1934.
101 Hancock & Weston, 155 & 313-6. Plumpton was aware of this venture: *Treasure Cruise*, 172.
102 *The Times*, 20 August 1934.
103 Hancock & Weston, 163; *Hartlepool Mail*, 20 August 1934.

British Crown, and hoisted the Union Jack upon arrival. As we have noted, he may have done this because he drew the wrong conclusion from the Peace Handbook's section on the ownership of the Island.

This first expedition had to be aborted when the chief engineer cracked his skull, was evacuated to Panama and died there! Captain Arthur wanted to continue, especially since he had left most of his crew on the Island; but the diplomatic chickens now came home to roost. The Panama Canal authorities impounded Arthur's ship for non-payment of tolls and duties, and the Costa Rican government barred him from returning to the Island. His Majesty's Government was asked to intervene, but declined to do so. The Costa Ricans sent two launches and 75 soldiers, who were lost at sea for a few days, but eventually arrived on Cocos, arrested 18 treasure hunters and confiscated all their equipment. Hearing of this, Drexel asked for his yacht back.[104]

At this point, Captain Arthur abandoned his ship and his men, and scuttled off back to England; but it is pleasant to report that his crew were all acquitted of any wrongdoing, since the Judge who heard the case thought that they had all been duped by their Captain.[105] 200 electric lamps which had been left on the Island were confiscated by the Costa Ricans and given to the penal colony on St Luke's Island, where members of Fitzwilliam's party had been so royally entertained in 1904. Arthur's crew were allowed to sail home on the *Queen of Scots*, returning to English shores at the end of November 1934.

Following this incident, it was reported that the Costa Ricans were about to establish a garrison, or perhaps a new penal colony, on Cocos Island. Foreigners would be kept out and no-one would ever again be allowed to exploit the Island's potential riches; but in the event, they did little more than issue postage stamps, 'with the avowed object of establishing her claim to the ownership of the treasure island of Cocos'.[106] The issuing of stamps became

---

104   *The Times*, 29 October 1934.
105   Hancock & Weston, Chapter 17; *The Times*, 29 October 1934.
106   *Sunderland Daily Echo and Shipping Gazette*, 9 October 1934; *Western Morning News*, 20 December 1934; *Yorkshire Post & Leeds Intelligencer*, 20 December 1934; *The Observer*, 10 November 1935; *The Times*, 21 February 1936.

a regular source of revenue thereafter. In 1964, a small post office was even established on the Island.[107]

Captain Arthur was not a man who was easily embarrassed and, amazingly, he managed to restore relations with various members of the 1934 expedition. He persuaded them that there had been a 'misunderstanding' with the Costa Ricans, but said that all would now be well, because he had done a deal with Clayton Metalophone and bought out its concession. New capital was raised, for a second expedition in 1935. Another ship was acquired, called the *Veracity* (an odd name in the circumstances). She set sail for Cocos Island on 11 February, without Captain Arthur; but those on board were in possession of new information. This had been supplied by Petrus Bergmans, a Belgian of dubious reputation who claimed to have been on the Island and discovered the treasure, but had been unable to take any of it away with him. The expeditionaries were at first suspicious: they thought his story was a mere ruse, to get money out of the company; but eventually, after sending a Captain Polkinghorne to interview Bergmans (who was by now in jail in Antwerp), they decided to recruit the Belgian after all. Following which, he disappeared.

Veracity reached Barbados on 23 April and Cocos Island on 9 June. The story now gets stranger and stranger. When she arrived at Cocos Island, the crew spotted four American 'castaways' already on the beach in Chatham Bay. They had been shipwrecked there in April 1935 after setting sail from California the previous December in the auxiliary sloop *Skukum* on a pleasure cruise bound for New York; but two of them now offered to stay on the Island 'to give the Britishers a helping hand.' Hancock and Weston, who later interviewed them in Costa Rica, thought they had in fact been on a treasure hunt of their own, especially since they did not appear to be hungry. This suspicion was confirmed when it was discovered that they not only had plenty of guns and ammunition on the island, as well as picks and shovels, and that they had been digging in various places.

Meanwhile, Bergmans had been found in a brothel in Puntarenas, and turned over by the police to the captain of the *Veracity*, which now returned to Cocos with him. There, he claimed to have found various places where

---

107 C.Weston has a photograph of this on page 143.

treasure was to be found; but it was not long before at least some of the search party concluded that he was a fraud.[108]

Not everyone was content with these developments. Some of Treasure Recovery's creditors asked the High Court in London to wind up the company, and their petition was granted in May 1936, leaving 1,500 creditors in the lurch.[109] Others took action against Captain Arthur personally, and this eventually resulted in his bankruptcy, in 1939. The assistant Official Receiver informed the creditors' meeting that Arthur could not be found, because he had now gone fishing in Trinidad.[110]

AMERICAN EXPEDITIONS

The great wealth of the United States, and its proximity to Costa Rica, meant that there were probably many more expeditions sent to Cocos Island from American ports in the 1920s and '30s than there were from ports in Great Britain; but again space permits us to look at only a few.

JULIUS FLEISCHMANN, 1931

Julius Fleischmann (known as 'Junkie') was a very wealthy man with a taste for adventure – the American equivalent of Earl Fitzwilliam, but an American tycoon rather than a British aristocrat. The following account appeared in an American magazine.[111]

JUNKIE'S BIG ADVENTURE

Charles Louis Fleischmann had grown up in Eastern Europe and apprenticed to a distiller and yeast maker before emigrating to Cincinnati in the 1860s, where he founded what became the Fleischmann Yeast

---
108 H&W, 214-248.
109 *The Times*, 9 July 1936.
110 *The Manchester Guardian*, 25 March 1939.
111 http://www.cincinnatimagazine.com/features/julius-fleischmann-jr-treasures-of-travel-geier-center/

Company in 1868. Charles Fleischmann's son, Julius, took over the family business at age 22 and invested in thoroughbred horses and baseball teams, including the Cincinnati *Shamrocks*, while also finding time to launch a political career.

In 1931 Fleischmann went on a world cruise on his 225-foot yacht *Camargo*, said to be the largest and most expensive pleasure craft of its day. She was a seaworthy beauty, with a clipper bow and sleek hull, a 60,000-gallon fuel tank, and two 800-horsepower Krupp diesel engines that could produce a cruising speed of 12 knots...

Julius Jr. also wrote a book in 1935 about the world cruise, *Footsteps in the Sea*. An entire chapter is devoted to Cocos Island off the west coast of Costa Rica, which Fleischmann had previously visited and had been surprised to find had no land birds.[112] Accordingly, he released some domesticated chickens, ducks, and geese on the Island, to see if they could survive there.

The landing party soon encountered another surprise: the makeshift hut of three castaways who had been stranded on the island for half a year. A note left behind by the starving men said they had travelled to another part of the island in search of coconuts.

"During our previous visits to Cocos we had been...to see the place where August Gissling had lived for twenty years while searching for the famous Cocos Island treasure...and it was to the ruins of his corrugated-iron huts that we were now headed to free our birds among coconut and lime groves which he had planted.

As we entered the bay, we noticed that the formerly ruined huts had been set up again and that two flags of the international code were flying on improvised staffs. As we landed on the beach we noticed fairly fresh footprints on the sand...We advanced cautiously, whistling and calling out to anyone who might be in the camp...

---

112 I doubt this, since ornithologists later found evidence of learning ability from studies of the Cocos Finch: *The Times*, 30 November 1987.

Attached to a clothes-line strung up inside the hut was a note...It read as follows:

Gentlemen: We (3) of us have gone around on the south side of the island to get cocoanuts as our supply here is very limited...We have been on here since April 15 and our supply of nuts and eats are very poor...We remain 3 hungry men trying to get to the canal zone. Please do not pass us up. We will return here about Nov. 4 or 5.

For a moment we were speechless...Just as we were about to return to *Camargo*, we remembered the object of our visit...the barnyard fowl...A sign was erected which announced to the world that they were placed on the island for experimental purposes, asked that they be protected and that word as to their progress be sent to me at Cincinnati.

It amused me to think of three starving men returning to their camp, reading the sign, seeing the birds, thumbing their noses at Julius Fleischmann and then sitting down to a delicious dinner... Back on board we fired four shots from our one-pounder and blew our whistle for prolonged periods...But the wind was against us and the rain so heavy that we were fairly sure our signals did not carry far enough to be heard. In the evening we held a council of war and decided to radio Admiral Irwin at Panama, telling him what we had discovered...and asked if he would therefore send us naval assistance to transport them to Panama."

So who were these shipwrecked sailors? A cable was filed in Balboa, Canal Zone, October 27, 1931, and appeared in several U. S. West Coast papers on the 28th:

Three American castaways, wearing nothing but loin cloths, were found on a beach of the lonely Pacific island of Cocos today by the United States gunboat *Sacramento* after they had lived a Robinson

Crusoe existence for six months. The refugees are Paul Stachwick of Huron, S. D.; Gordon Brawner of Springfield, Ill., and Elmer J. Palliser of San Diego, Calif. They were shipwrecked April 15, the rescue ship reported by radio. Tonight they are on their way to Balboa. Until they were first found by a searching party from the yacht *Camargo*... they had lived on coconuts, fish and wild pig, they said. The three men were sighted this afternoon by the *Sacramento*, which had been sent out from Balboa to search for them.[113]

CHARLES M. WILKINS, 1938

Captain Charles M. Wilkins, of Long Beach, California, travelled to Cocos Island on his 150-ton auxiliary schooner, *San Pedro,* in February and March, 1938. Back in California, he had been approached by a young fellow by the name of Milton Canham, who had a tale to tell, similar to the yarn spun by Petrus Bergmans.

Canham said that, a few years previously, while he had been visiting Cocos Island with some friends from California, he had accidentally stumbled on the treasure cache. He had even carried away with him a part of the treasure when he eventually left the island, and he was now looking for someone to bear the expense of an expedition to go to Cocos to recover the rest.

Wilkins was interested in Canham's tale. He checked it as far as he could, and he discovered that round about the time indicated, Canham had actually disposed of a substantial quantity of pure gold. Wilkins then formed a private syndicate with some friends to pool the expenses of the expedition and Canham was given several hundred dollars in cash as an advance on his share of the treasure. They sailed from California on February 20th and in due course arrived at Puntarenas, where Wilkins obtained formal permission to visit Cocos.

Less than two weeks after leaving Puntarenas, Wilkins & Co. were back again in Puntarenas. His first action on reaching port was to have young Canham locked up in the local jail on a charge of obtaining money under

---

113 H&W, Appendix IX; see also.

false pretences. Then he went up to San José and told his story to the U.S. consul. Canham, he said, was a fraud. He had brought Wilkins and his friends all the way from California on a fool's errand.

> "Why, the very moment we stepped ashore on Cocos, we knew that Canham had never even seen the island before. He was completely lost and didn't know which way to turn. His story about having been there before and finding the treasure was a lot of bunk. And then he had the nerve to laugh it off as a good joke."[114]

JAMES ALEXANDER FORBES IV, 1939-60

As for Charles and James Forbes, of whom the Foreign Office professed to know nothing in 1949, these two brothers were the descendants of James Alexander Forbes I, whose remarkable career forms a central part of Hancock and Weston's book *The Lost Treasure of Cocos Island*, (New York, 1960). James was in fact James Alexander Forbes IV.

The first of the dynasty supposedly served as first mate to Captain Thompson, on board the *Mary Dear*, and indeed (according to Hancock and Weston) played a more important role than the Captain, in taking the Treasure of Lima out of the port of Callao and burying it on Cocos Island in 1821. Forbes had then become a prominent figure in Californian public life, but had done nothing with his charts and papers, except to pass them on to his son, and so on down the line, to J.A.Forbes IV, before anyone got up an expedition to retrieve great-grand-father's ill-gotten gains.

Hancock and Weston swallowed this wild tale whole; but when the Frenchman Robert Vergnes came to write his second book on the subject in 1978, he expressed some scepticism. Vergnes thought it unlikely that a secret as big as the one which it was said that J.A. Forbes I had, would have descended over three generations before anyone acted on it. He told how J.A. Forbes III had been asked about the long silence, and had replied that none of his ancestors had ever had the money to pursue the idea, which seems unlikely,

---

114 H&W, 285-6

since the Forbeses had prospered in California, at least until the Great Crash of 1929. At any rate, J.A. Forbes III eventually agreed to back a treasure hunt, at the suggestion of Douglas Narron; and the two had even agreed to share the profits to be derived from the venture, and hired a vessel, *The Spindrift*, in 1938; but then Forbes died, bequeathing the project to his son, the fourth of that name.[115]

J.A. Forbes IV made seven or eight journeys to Cocos Island between 1939 and 1960; but once again, never found anything of value,[116] despite having the best American technology at his disposal. There is one photograph in particular which shows a team of five men at the base of a pit, which is about twenty feet deep, and about the same in diameter. The pit is entirely surrounded by a double sheet of what appears to be corrugated iron, shored up with timber. This is not the sort of structure which could have been erected cheaply or quickly. It involved the use of expensive excavating equipment, which must have been shipped to the Island.[117]

A GERMAN EXPEDITION

COUNT LUCKNER, 1937

Gissler had no followers; but he may well have inspired Felix Graf von Luckner (1881 – 1966), who was a German nobleman and naval officer who earned the epithet *Der Seeteufel* (the Sea-Devil) for his exploits during the First World War, while in command of S.M.S. *Seeadler* (*Sea Eagle*). Luckner had become a hero on both sides, for successfully waging war without heavy casualties.

In 1926 Luckner raised funds to buy a sailing ship which he called the *Vaterland* ('Fatherland') and set out on a goodwill mission around the world. An entertaining speaker, he was widely admired and addressed large audiences

---

115 Vergnes (1978), chapter 32.
116 H&W, 272-291.
117 Vergnes (1978), photo between pp 192 and 193.

in the United States. In 1937 and 1938, he and his wife undertook a round-the-world voyage in his yacht *Seeteufel*. They were welcomed in New Zealand and Australia, although some viewed him as a mere apologist for the Nazis.

While sailing across the Pacific Luckner anchored off Cocos Island and made what Rollo Gebner described as a 'not very serious attempt' to find 'the great treasure of the Island.' The Count himself described the attractions of the Island

> One thing the greedy pirates of our world bequeathed to us is a real piece of romance. Even in a hundred years' time, boys' hearts will beat faster when the great treasure of Cocos Island is mentioned. They will make plans, and each one of them will believe that he can achieve the impossible.

We are reminded of Mark Twain's remark:

> There comes a time in every rightly constructed boy's life when he has a raging desire to go somewhere and dig for buried treasure.

Chapter 8

THE SCEPTIC

THE 'CRUISE OF THE *ALERTE*'

We have seen that the period between the World Wars was the heyday of treasure-hunting on Cocos Island; but there is no sign that any of these latter-day adventurers found anything, any more than their predecessors had done, despite the widespread use of new technology. Their repeated, and sometimes disreputable, failure may have helped to create a new mood of scepticism, at least among the reading public, especially when E.F. Knight's account of his cruise on the *Alerte*, first published in 1891, was re-published in 1929, in The Nautilus Library.

In 1889 Knight (1852-1925) sailed from Southampton to an island named Trinidad, in the South Atlantic – not the Trinidad of Trinidad & Tobago, but a small island with an area of 3.9 square miles, which belonged, then as now, to Brazil. Like Cocos Island, Trinidad Island is volcanic, but also largely barren. Knight had originally come across it in 1881, when he landed there during a cruise in the South Atlantic;[118] but it was only after his return that he first learned of a fabulous story concerning buried treasure, which was supposedly to be found there. Three years later, in 1888, he heard the full story from a group of men in the North-East of England.

---

118 His account of that voyage was in due course published as *The Cruise of the 'Falcon'*.

There is now living, not far from Newcastle, a retired sea captain, Captain P--, who was in command of an East Indiaman engaged in the opium trade in the years 1848 to 1850. At that time the China seas were infested by pirates, so that his vessel carried a few guns, and a larger crew than is usual in these days. He had four quartermasters, one of whom was a foreigner. Captain P-- is not sure of his nationality, but thinks he was a Russian Finn. On board the vessel the man went under the name of 'the pirate,' on account of a deep scar across his cheek, which gave him a somewhat sinister appearance.

Captain P-- took a liking to him, and showed him kindness on various occasions. This man was attacked by dysentery on the voyage from China to Bombay. When he was dying he told Captain P--, who frequently visited him at the hospital, that he felt very grateful for the kind treatment he had receive, and that he would prove his gratitude by revealing a secret to him that might make him one of the richest men in England. He then asked Captain P-- to go to his chest and take out from it a parcel. The parcel contained a piece of old tarpaulin with a plan of the island of Trinidad on it.

The man gave him this plan, and told him that at the place indicated on it - that is, under the mountain known as the Sugarloaf - there was an immense treasure buried, consisting principally of gold and silver plate and ornaments, the plunder of Peruvian churches which certain pirates had concealed there in the year 1821. Much of this plate, he said, came from the cathedral of Lima, having been carried away from there during the War of Independence, when the Spaniards were escaping the country, and that among other riches there were several massive golden candlesticks.[119]

Of course, this is a completely different story from the one we have heard about Cocos Island; but it is about Peruvian treasure, and date of 1821 is by now familiar. Whether it is any more credible than the numerous tales about

---

119 Knight, 13-15.

Thompson and the *Mary Dear*, is for the reader to judge; but certainly Knight believed it; and he gave his reasons.

> In the first place the archives of Cuba were inspected, and a record was discovered which showed that a gang of pirates who had plundered Spanish vessels sailing from Lima had been hanged at Havannah at the time mentioned.
>
> The probability of the story *is* further strengthened by the actual history of Peru during the War of Independence. It appears that the Spanish population of Lima entertained a wholesome dread of the liberators of their country, and deposited large sums of money and a vast amount of plate' in the forts for security.[120]

Knight then gives an account of the Peruvian Revolution. In doing so, he relies heavily on the *Narrative of Services* of Lord Cochrane; and in particular he emphasizes Cochrane's command of the sea in 1821. His explanation for his belief that pirates were nevertheless able to smuggle a large amount of treasure out of Callao, appears to be the same as that given by Hancock & Weston in relation to the *Mary Dear* in 1960: that Cochrane could not keep watch on every vessel which used the port of Lima; but no hard evidence of any piratical raid is produced; and in any case, the pirate in question was the mysterious Captain P--, not Captain Thompson, while the name of P--'s vessel is nowhere stated.

In 1889, Knight selected a crew of around ten men, from 150 who responded to an advert in the *St James's Magazine*, and found the *Alerte*, a cutter-yacht built in 1864, 64.3 feet in length, 14.5 feet by the beam and 9 feet deep. They took rifles, revolvers and a whaling-gun, 'a complete set of equipment which would enable them to bore through rock and earth to a depth of 50 feet, and a hydraulic jack, capable of lifting twelve tons. They also took shovels, picks, crowbars, iron wheelbarrows, carpenter's and other tools, a portable forge and anvil, and other materials for timbering a shaft. Notwithstanding

---

120 Knight, 15-17.

the careful preparation, the expedition had no success. (Nor did any subsequent expedition to Trinidad Island).

Nevertheless, Knight did not conclude that there never had been any treasure on Trinidad Island. At the end of his book, he wrote that he was often asked whether he believed in its existence.

> Knowing all I do, I have very little doubt that the story of the Russian Finn is substantially true - that the treasures of Lima were hidden on Trinidad; but whether they have been taken away, or whether they are still there and we failed to find them because we were not in possession of one link in the directions, I am unable to say.

When he read Knight's account, Admiral Chambers (see below) concluded:

> It was interesting to discover that the Trinidad treasure, probably the most notable cache after that of Cocos Island, had a similar origin and was actually of the same date, namely 1821.

Personally, I find the coincidence more than 'interesting', I think that what we have found here was another nail in the coffin of the myth concerning Cocos Island. We have already seen that the versions of the myth which were current in the U.S.A. were quite different from the British; but at least they were concerned with how a vast hoard of treasure came to be buried on Cocos. Here, we have Knight telling us that the most famous hoard of all – the Treasure of Lima no less, not the *Devonshire* treasure, or Benito Bonito's or anyone else's – had been taken to a different island, in a different Ocean altogether, and not by Captain Thompson, nor on the *Mary Dear*.

CAPTAIN WHALL

Captain W.B.Whall was a master mariner, the author of a *Handy Book of the Stars* and a co-author of *Merchant Seamanship*. He also wrote *Sea Songs and Shanties,* and *The Romance of Navigation* (1932), which has a chapter on

'Hidden Treasure'. This includes a section which deals both with Trinidad Island and with Cocos Island.[121]

So far as Trinidad Island is concerned, Whall had read Knight's book, and (contrary to what Knight himself thought) he was scathing about the chances of any treasure ever being found there.

> At least five expeditions have been made with the object of recovering this treasure, but without result. Mr. Knight's party carried on systematic digging for several months, and only desisted when satisfied that further search was useless. Trinidad is an uninviting place, subject to earthquakes and volcanic disturbances, which have caused numerous landslips and blasted most of the trees. Its most unpleasant feature is that it is infested with huge land crabs of disgusting appearance, which are popularly believed to have eaten alive certain unfortunates marooned there in former times. If any treasure was ever deposited on the island, it is probable that all traces were covered up long ago by landslips.[122]

As for Cocos Island, Whall starts by telling us to be wary.

> According to one account, the first treasure was deposited about the year 1821 by the crew of a British ship who had become pirates. It was very carefully hidden by sinking in gravel and tunnelling in rock. Subsequently the pirate leaders were captured, tried and executed, the rest of the crew being sentenced to various terms of imprisonment. There is no chart to show the whereabouts of the spoil, every clue that has been followed in efforts to find it having been evolved from the memories of the few who did not pay the full penalty of their exploits. They retailed scraps of the story to their friends, and now, owing to the lapse of time, any particle of reliable evidence that may have existed has vanished.

---

121 Whall, 217-224.
122 Whall, 218-9.

Then we have this.

> The second and most important treasure is supposed to have been deposited on Cocos Island by the crew of the British barquentine *Mary Dier* [sic], about the year 1835. To the master and crew of this vessel were entrusted the treasures of the Peruvian port of Callao, threatened with sack by a revolutionary army. The timely arrival in the harbour of the British vessel suggested to the Governor of the city the somewhat risky plan of placing the municipal treasures on board for safety. The temptation proved too great, and the *Mary Dier* decamped with the valuables, which they buried on the island. The value of the cache is said to have been equal to some millions sterling. Two members of the barquentine's crew were named Thomson [sic] and Keating.

This garbled account seems to confuse the first treasure with the second, in addition to getting the name of the ship and its captain wrong. The fact is that there was no revolution in Peru in 1835. Further, Whall's version of events confuses a royal Viceroy with a republican Governor; and lastly, no-one has ever suggested before that Keating was on board the *Mary Dear*, or *Dier*. He usually shows up years later, in Newfoundland.

Perhaps Whall felt that it did not matter whether he reproduced these stories accurately, because they were only 'yarns' (his word). There was only a fragment of truth in any of them, and they were more suitable as material for the writers of fiction, like Edgar Allan Poe and Robert Louis Stevenson, than a source for the serious historian. However, it is noticeable that Whall's account of later voyages and expeditions which undoubtedly did take place, is equally inaccurate. For example:

> After returning to England Admiral Palliser induced Earl Fitzwilliam to fit out an expedition, equipped with up-to-date plant for cutting away the tangled undergrowth of the Cocos wilderness, and blasting the rock supposed to cover the treasure cave. At the same time that Lord Fitzwilliam was making these preparations, one Harold Grey,

> who presumably derived his information from another source, quietly departed in his steam yacht *Rose Marie* for Panama, and was at the island before the Palliser-Fitzwilliam party had crossed the Atlantic. When the latter arrived, there was a stand-up fight between the rival bands of treasure seekers.

This simply isn't right, as we can tell from the accounts of Fitzwilliam's expedition by David Smith (1932) and George Cooke-Yarborough (unpublished). While Fitzwilliam did encounter Harold Gray, this was in Costa Rica, not Cocos Island, and there was no fight. Whall has simply believed some of the wilder stories he read in the Press.[123]

Whall had also read Montmorency's *On the Track of A Treasure* (1904) and believed every word.

> Before the last-mentioned abortive expeditions, there had been one in 1903 led by a certain Captain Shrapnel, who apparently claimed to have been a British naval officer, though his name is not to be found in any Navy list of the period. With him was associated a gentleman who rejoiced in the name of Hervey de Montmorency, the author of a graphic account of the adventure. The treasure seekers numbered seven in all, their vessel's name being the *Lytton*.

The important point here, as we know, is that 'Captain Shrapnel' never existed. Montmorency was writing about Admiral Palliser.

Whall was also poorly-informed about August Gissler.

> Before leaving [the adventurers] visited a man named Gissler who is stated to have lived a solitary life in this tropical island for sixteen years. During his residence he had erected one or two huts of corrugated iron, set back a little from the beach, with plantations and cultivated patches all about them.

---

123 See Cooper & Moorhouse, EFTI, 2016.

This scarcely does justice to a man who spent 18 years on Cocos Island, and built substantial wooden buildings there, as well as engaging in subsistence farming, and excavating extensive tunnels, with the aid of his small colony of German settlers. However, Whall redeems himself when he makes the following speculation.

> The question has sometimes been raised whether the whole story of the treasure was not evolved in the fertile brain of Keating or Hackett as a modification of the well- known ' Spanish prisoner' hoax.

Now this is the second time that we have seen it suggested that the story regarding the Cocos Island Treasure was a variant of the Spanish prisoner confidence trick; but, having put the question, Captain Whall does not answer it.

Our next writer did not directly accuse anyone of perpetrating a fraud or hoax; but he does provide evidence that some treasure-hunters, and especially those who floated limited companies, made promises which they must have known they would be unable to keep.

ADMIRAL CHAMBERS

Bertram Mordaunt Chambers, C.B., (1866 - 1945) was a distinguished naval officer who served in the First World War. Like Palliser, he was only advanced to the rank of Admiral after he retired. In February 1935 he published an article in *Chambers's Journal*, the successor to *Chambers's Edinburgh Journal*, which had been started in 1832. (Magazines had become much more numerous and popular after 1900, both in the U.S.A. and Britain, thanks to increasing literacy rates, the growth of advertising, and the consequent fall in their price). Chambers's article posed a question: *Did the Cocos Island Treasure Exist?* And the answer, noted by *The Times* the same month, was an unambiguous 'No.'[124]

---

[124] *The Times*, 1 February 1935. The review was very short: 'Admiral Chambers disputes the existence at any time of the Cocos Island treasure and of the ship *Mary Dier*.'

Chambers started by explaining that he had long been 'a student' of treasure and pirate's literature, but thought that the popularity of the gentre had been exploited by the unscrupulous, who had used it as a lure to attract 'a certain type of investor.'

> For beyond the human desire for gain lies the hope that by proxy, at least, the investor may share in some glorious adventure redeeming the dullness of modern day life.

The Admiral had spent many years at sea and his considered advice, in old age, to anyone drawn to such 'enterprises' was clear.

> They should all be treated with gravest suspicion. The treasure-seeker should remember that for years after piratical enterprises had ceased, the old sailor with a treasure-chart was a familiar character at every maritime port. Such stories were a very profitable variant of the 'Spanish treasure' fraud, and there is no doubt that it was in this way that many of these legends originated.

On reading this, it is safe to conclude that Chambers was thinking of the prospectuses issued by Cocos Island Treasure Ltd and Treasure Recovery Ltd in the early 1930s (though the reader may recall that, as early as 1911, Paine had referred to an 'elaborate' prospectus relating to Cocos Island); and we cannot help wondering if so many people would have lost their money, if they had but taken the Admiral's advice. Would they even have considered that the investment they were being asked to make was a 'glorious adventure', if they had known that it was more of a tacky confidence trick? Chambers gave other reasons for doubting the promises made to investors.

> Even if we assume that some of the stories may be based on fact, the possibility that previous searches may have taken place must be considered, for the successful treasure-seeker does not, as a rule, parade his success before the eyes of the world. The treasure may thus

have been recovered long ago; indeed, one naval officer who took part in a classical attempt at Cocos Island was definitely of that opinion. Again, in civilised surroundings and with the backing of documents which may appear to be ancient and genuine - a cross, perhaps, marked upon a tiny plan to indicate the place of burial - there will be induced a very different frame of mind in the seeker than when he is confronted with broad hill-sides whose ravines have been washed by the rains of a hundred years, where forests have grown up and decayed in their tropical luxuriance, season after season, since the tall ship landed those heavy chests of treasure.

Chambers then divulged that he had himself become an 'adventurer' to the extent of investing five dollars in a company which proposed an expedition, due to leave for Cocos Island from Vancouver in Canada in 1933. Although he does not name the company, this must have been Campbell's Cocos Island Treasure Limited.[125] In view of what he has said about the nature of such enterprises, Chambers feels obliged to offer the following excuse for investing even a modest amount.

> It was with the intent of obtaining a report of the doings of the expedition than with any idea of gain that I made my investment, for I had already formed a very definite idea of the hoard's non-existence. I was, however, disappointed even in my modest hopes, for beyond a suggestion that the treasure was on the point of recovery in the early days, I heard nothing, and no report came to hand of how our money was expended,

Chambers thought that the story of the Treasure of Lima, which he regarded as 'the star turn' among treasure and pirate tales, had only come into prominence in 1898. It was in that year that Palliser obtained the information which led him to divert his ship *Impérieuse* on that unofficial visit to Cocos Island. As an Admiral himself, Chambers could readily understand the Royal

---

125 C.Weston, 66-7.

Navy's displeasure, but pointed out that Palliser 'cared little or nothing for their lordships' possible reprimand.' However, what he could not understand was 'the horrible slur' thrown by the traditional legend 'upon the character of the British seaman.' What did he mean by this?

Chambers had read Campbell's book; and he reproduced the latter's highly fictionalised account of Captain Thompson's treacherous dealings with the Viceroy of Peru. This included the following paragraph, concerning the aftermath of Thompson's seizure of the treasure at Callao.

> Late that night Captain Thompson and his men burst open the cabin doors of their passengers and cut their throats as they slept. It was a butchery of the most disgusting order, with none of the bravery of victory in pitched battle to redeem it. We can think more kindly of Morgan's torturings by rack and fire in Panama than of Captain Thompson's murders.

It was this foul deed, supposedly committed by a member of the British (merchant) navy, which made Chambers smell a rat. He simply could not believe that a fellow countryman of his, and a naval man at that, could have been guilty of conduct like this; and he set out to prove that the whole story was a myth.

Chambers had been stationed in Callao in 1883 and again ten years later. He knew the port well, and had talked to many Peruvians about naval history and shipping in general. What struck him was that he

> had never heard even a whisper of this horrible massacre, though the Peruvian was generally quite willing to recount other affairs which he considered to the discredit of the British nation.

Chambers also concluded that key features of Campbell's version of events, whilst making a 'capital story', were inaccurate. So, Campbell had written that

> [The] Lima of that day was a city of unbelievable riches. Her banks were stored with bullion, her cathedrals and churches were full of

solid gold images, her inhabitants dined off gold and silver plate, and her traders and nobility were millionaires. We may imagine the scene, under the torrid blue skies of that South American day, with the spire of that great cathedral upthrust above the roofs of the white houses and the narrow streets, alive with anxious jostling crowds. Then, forcing a passage through them, comes a long line of pack-mules carrying bullion from the banks, solid bars of gold, the jewels and plate of the chief inhabitants, and finally, in two great wooden boxes, the gold Virgin and Child from the cathedral.

Now, Chambers knew Lima (whilst Campbell never visited it); and he was able to say with authority that

> the streets are far from narrow and the cathedral has no spire. Like the majority of Spanish American ecclesiastical buildings, it has two prominent towers.

Chambers had also read Knight's *Cruise of the Alerte* and Whall's *Romance of Navigation*; and found that neither of them provided him with any good reason for believing in the traditional legend: on the contrary they confirmed his initial scepticism. He also studied materials relating to the Peruvian Revolution, and came to the view that it was unnecessary to introduce Captain Thompson, as a kind of *deus ex machina*, to explain the disappearance of the wealth of Peru in 1821. This could perfectly well be explained by other factors.

> The city was threatened by General San Martin in 1821.[126] In that year Captain Basil Hall, R.N., was upon the coast in H.M.S. *Conway*. His well-known journal was written of the years 1820, '21, '22, and he was actually at Callao at the time of its occupation by San Martin. We get a very full account of what then really took place. We find from his journal that the treasures of Lima, instead of being put on board ship, British or otherwise, were sent away into the interior,

---

126 Not Bolivar, as Campbell would have us believe.

and there is more than a hint in his account that British merchant vessels would not have been welcome in the port until after the city's capture by the patriots - for Captain Hall describes the roads as then crowded with shipping, and makes comparison with their deserted condition on a previous visit. It is probable that, with Cochrane in the offing, Spanish treasure would in any case have been considered far from safe afloat.

One can hardly imagine such an energetic and money-loving personality as Cochrane permitting some seven or eight millions in gold and silver to be spirited off from under his nose - even by a brother Scot. Neither he nor Basil Hall makes any mention of piratical excursions, though it is almost certain that they would have done so had any big affair taken place at that time.

Chambers was very thorough. He turned up another witness, relating to the suggestion that Thompson had carried away the Madonna of Lima.

It so happens that another British man-of-war was on the coast a little earlier, H.M.S. *Briton*. She was at Callao in the year 1818, and the marine officer, one Shellibear, not only visited the cathedral at Lima, but wrote a very full account of its riches. It is as follows:

'The cathedral does not possess any external beauty, but the splendour, magnificence and riches of the interior can alone be conceived. The enchanted palaces as described in fairy-tales recurred to my memory the instant I entered this elegant sanctuary. The great altar at the eastern end is modern and the columns numerous; they are, together with every other part, covered with silver about the thickness of a dollar, and when lit up for the performance of any particular ceremony, its brilliant and beautiful appearance cannot be exceeded.'

So, the fabulous Madonna was just that – a fable! However, Chambers now made further enquiries at the Peruvian Consulate in London.

Having obtained from these sources at least a fair presumption that the story of the *Mary Dier* was an invention, I made inquiry of the Peruvian Consul-General, who should certainly be in a position to know whether such an international happening had ever taken place. I was here confronted with a somewhat unexpected difficulty - repeated letters met with no response, and it was not until I paid a personal visit to the Consulate, explaining that I was in no sense a treasure-seeker, that I obtained a full reply to my questions.

No! As I had suspected, nothing whatever was known in Peru either of the ship or the piracy. I did gather, however, that the Consulate was very thoroughly bored with the whole affair - though I personally met with every courtesy, more especially when the secretary discovered that I was acquainted with his home town, Piura, some sixty miles by rail from the little port of Payta, so often sacked by British buccaneers.

As far as the Consulate was aware, the only piratical affair in which a British ship had taken part was one in which the treasure involved had nothing about it so spectacular as seven or eight millions. I would find, he said, that the story was written in a book, *Tradiciones Peruanas,* by one Ricardo Palma. The author was a Peruvian gentleman and a writer of some note in the later part of last century, a voracious collector of all unusual and romantic happenings in the story of Peru. The piracy which he recorded belonged to the year 1826, and curiously enough the Captain *was* a Scotsman, and a Captain Thompson was mixed up in the affair.

What can we make of this suggestion? Ricardo Palma (1833 – 1919) was a Peruvian author, scholar, librarian and politician. His book *Tradiciones Peruanas* ('Peruvian Traditions'), which consisted of more than 500 stories, was a series, published between 1872 and 1910, and amongst the first stories to be published was a tale entitled *Dos Milliones* ('Two Millions'), which was indeed concerned with an episode of piracy; and we should note that, although this story in the early 1870s, half a century after the Peruvian Revolution, this did coincide with H.M.S.O.s start date for the better-documented treasure-hunting expeditions.

According to *Dos Milliones*, 1826 was a time of 'great agitation' in Lima and Callao; and a Scotsman called Robertson took advantage of this, recruiting a crew of roughnecks to assist him in stealing a large quantity of treasure, which included gold coin and silver plate, and placing it on board an English brig called *The Peruvian*. Now, at this point we should say that Robertson bears little resemblance to Captain William Thompson, apart (possibly) from being Scots, and apart from the fact that he takes command of an English brig in Callao. The treasure is certainly not 'the great Treasure of Lima', Robertson has no mate, and his reason for stealing the treasure has less to do with revolution, than with greed and personal ambition. We are told briefly how he had fallen in love with a society lady called Teresa Méndez, who had rejected him, by saying she could never love a man who was not 'a commander'. Having taken command of the *Peruvian*, Robertson evaded those sent to pursue him, eliminated numerous potential rivals who formed part of his villainous crew and succeeded in burying the treasure on the island of Agrigan. This is a real island in the Pacific, but it is at the opposite end of the Pacific from Cocos Island, in the Marianas – in fact, nearer to Japan than South America. Subsequently, Robertson travelled to Rio de Janeiro in Brazil and Hobart in Tasmania; and it was only now that he met an ancient English captain (of a fishing vessel), called Thompson. For a while, Robertson and Thompson became partners; but at long last, the long arm of the law caught up with them, in the shape of a Spanish frigate. Thompson was arrested, but Robertson escaped and evaded arrest a while longer. Eventually though, he too was apprehended; but rather than face justice, he threw himself overboard, taking his secrets with him.

Now, plainly, this story is fiction, though the civil servant who told it to Chambers seems to have regarded it as fact; but the important point is that he did so only for the purpose of demonstrating that there was no evidence for the truth of traditional British legend regarding Thompson, the *Mary Dear*, and the supposed seizure of 'the Treasure of Lima' in 1821. This story of

Palma's was, according to the Admiral's informant, 'the *only* piratical affair in which a British ship had taken part', in that period.

Following his visit to the Consulate, Chambers set out to see if he could find any original sources confirming the existence of the *Mary Dear*.

> A visit to the reading-room at the British Museum[127] enabled me to acquire the details, and as such a thrilling story as the *Mary Dier* affair could certainly never have escaped such a painstaking historian, I can only conclude that the episode is mythical.
>
> Since writing the foregoing I have received information that neither Lloyds nor the Registrar of Shipping knows anything of a ship of the name *Mary Dier*, which confirms the belief that she never existed.[128]

Although Chambers used moderate language, his article is really a devastating criticism of the myth of the Treasure of Lima; and, although he did not use the phrase, it is also a condemnation of the kind of treasure-hunting which took place in the 1930s as a kind of 'casino capitalism'.

NESMITH & SNOW

Two books of stories about treasure and treasure-hunting were published in 1958, one in the U.S.A. and one in Britain; and, interestingly, the chapters on Cocos Island were each written from a sceptical point of view. Thus in *Dig for Pirate Treasure*, Nesmith points out (as Chambers had done) that, in the 1920s and 1930s there had been a 'treasure boom' in London, during which articles appeared regularly in the national newspapers about pirates, 'Captain Shrapnel', Benito Bonito, Captain Thompson and the *Mary Dier*; and also about 'syndicates' or limited companies which issued more or less misleading prospectuses to the public.

---

127 The contents are now in the British Library.
128 Confirmed by my own enquiries.

Nesmith more or less accuses the promoters of such companies of fraud, when he quotes a headline in the *Daily Mail*, which ran:

TREASURE HUNT BUNKUM
WARNING TO THE PUBLIC
DO NOT SUBSCRIBE[129]

E.R.Snow's *True Tales of Pirates and their gold* was also published in 1958. In Chapter XIV (entitled *The Loot of Lima*) the author openly advised his readers not to hope for any financial reward if they went treasure-hunting. This would only be worthwhile if they went in for it with their eyes wide-open, and 'for the fun of it.' He also wrote "My story will not please all my readers for I shall prove false many generally accepted beliefs concerning this tropical paradise".[130] Snow goes on say:

> Not one of the many writers who mention the incident of Captain Thompson and the *Mary Dear* admits having done research work to see if the man or ship ever existed. Actually, there never was a Captain Thompson of the period who visited Cocos Island, no one of that name ever had a vessel called the *Mary Dear*, and neither he nor anyone else ever took the so-called Loot of Lima. Records at Lima reveal no robbery of that sort at the time.[131]

---

129 Nesmith, 243.
130 Snow, 195-6.
131 Snow, 202-3.

Chapter 9

THE PERUVIAN REVOLUTION

One might have thought that these critiques, and especially Admiral Chambers's return to the sources, would have exploded the myth of the Treasure of Lima once and for all; but this was very far from being the case. Instead, it revived after the Second World War, and in some ways has gone from strength to strength. Yet, as Chambers pointed out, there was an alternative explanation for the disappearance of the wealth of Lima in 1821, the year of the Peruvian Revolution.

There is no doubt that pre-revolutionary Lima was home to various treasures. We see evidence of this wealth in the 'View of South America and Mexico', published by "A Citizen of the United States" in New York in 1826.

> [Lima is] the great emporium of trade for the whole Pacific coast of the continent of America, and the grand depot of the metallic regions of South America, into which [the Spaniards] have been pouring their wealth for nearly three centuries.

Spanish control of Central and South America was fatally undermined by Napoleon's intervention in the Iberian peninsula in 1808; and revolution broke out in Peru in 1811; but there were many setbacks, and no rapid transfer of power. Even when Lima was liberated, there were several changes of regime between 1821 and 1826, when Spanish rule finally came to an end. In these circumstances there were long months of uncertainty and even anarchy in the city, which were particularly worrying for the propertied classes and the Church, as well as for the Spanish Viceroy. This was potentially favourable territory for adventurers and pirates, as well as a breeding ground of rumour and legend; but the main facts can nonetheless be ascertained, from sources written in Spanish and in English.

SPANISH SOURCES

TWO VICEROYS
There were two Spanish Viceroys in Peru in 1821, not one, as the myth would have us believe. The first was Joaquín González de la Pezuela (1761 - 1830), who was deposed by his own side in January that year. The second was José de la Serna (1770 - 1832) who was forced to abandon the capital in July; but there is no mention, in the history of the careers of these two men, of their doing a deal with anyone to take the Treasure of Lima to a place of safety.

La Pezuela himself wrote extensively; but there is no mention of 'the Treasure of Lima', or of Captain William Thompson, or of the *Mary Dear*, in his memoir *El Gobierno*. His successor de la Serna has left no memoirs. However an excellent, and extremely well-researched and documented biography has recently appeared, written by a descendant who is a noted historian.

This biography tells us that Viceroy de la Serna deliberately decided to abandon Lima in as orderly a way as possible, and not to engage in a scorched-earth policy. However, he did take steps to transfer what he called both the most essential items (*lo mas necesario*) and 'the belongings of the V.I.P.s' (*las pertinencias de los particulares*) to the port of Callao. Later, after the rebel general San Martin had taken control of the capital, La Serna authorised the Royalist General Canterac to make an assault on Callao, in the hope of relieving the beleaguered port. This mission was not accomplished, but Canterac was able to enter Callao and retreat unmolested with certain armaments. La Serna also tells us in the clearest terms that 'the money, plate and gold in Callao, both that which belonged to the state and that which belonged to private citizens, was taken to neutral ships in the port of Ancón.' Finally, he tells us that Cochrane made off with 'all the wealth' in Ancón (*todos esos caudales*), in order to pay his men.[132] As we shall see, this is extremely important confirmation of what Admiral Cochrane himself had to say.

If either de la Pezuela or de la Serna had done a deal with Thompson, someone would surely have said something about it, when things went wrong. But, in fact, we know that both men were allowed to return to Spain, where they lived out an honourable retirement. Moreover, there is no sign of any investigation into their conduct, either in Spain, or by one of the many post-revolutionary governments in Peru.

TWO REVOLUTIONARIES

Two of the revolutionaries wrote about their experiences. Unfortunately, the Correspondence of José de San Martín (Protector of Peru between July 1821 and September 1822) only begins in 1823. However, José de la Riva Agüero, who was 5th President between February and June 1823, wrote his lengthy *Memorias y documentos para la Historia de la Independencia del Perú y causas del mal éxito que ha tenido ésta* ('Memories and documents for the history of the independence of Peru and causes for its failure so far'), though he only published this in 1858.

Agüero is very critical of his old comrade San Martin; but the smoking gun is to be found in Chapter Two. Here he makes no mention of 'the Treasure of Lima' but he does describe in some detail how San Martin stole a great part of the wealth that was in Peru in 1821.

In his *Vindication*, and in the repost he made to San Martin, Lord Cochrane said that [San Martin] had arranged for a vast hoard of

---

132 La Serna, 301, 307, 210, 313.

money to be place on board his own schooner the *Sacramento*, in place of ballast, considering it to be his own private property, and that in addition, there were seven sacks of uncoined gold brought down on his account by the legate Paroissien, with the intention of placing them on board the brigantine *Rebecca*. Each sack contained 3,000 ounces of gold, that is to say that the seven sacks contained 21,000 ounces of gold in all. And this sum did not include the gold and silver plate which was taken on board the *Sacramento* in place of ballast.

Looking at the hoard which San Martin had on board the schooner *Sacramento*, we can get an idea of how much he had extracted from Peru to that date, and of how much he managed to extract thereafter. And he had not just got away with a hoard for himself, he had also arranged for the removal of other property on behalf of others, thereby contributing to the size of the robbery. Where did all this treasure come from? There must have been 350,000 pesos contained in those seven sacks [put on the *Sacramento*], but it is certain that this must have been only a small part of what San Martin had taken out of Peru and had stowed away in Pisco, Ancón, Huacho etc. And this is the man who called himself Protector of Peru! [133]

The Spanish sources we have examined therefore provide no evidence for the existence of Captain Thompson, or the *Mary Dear*, or the taking of any treasure to Cocos Island. It is worth adding that none of these is mentioned in the collection of contemporary documents put together in 1971 by Ruben Vargas Uguarte of the Society of Jesus – a society well known in modern times for its thoroughness in matters of scholarship.[134]

SOURCES IN ENGLISH

Chambers's account of the Peruvian Revolution was ground-breaking, though few seemed to pay much attention to it at the time; but it was largely based on

---

133 Aguero, 59-60. My translation.
134 The collection mentions General Canterac, but not his raid on Lima in 1821.

one English source, the account of Basil Hall R.N. Fortunately, we can now pursue Chambers's investigation further, since there is an excellent summary of several contemporary English accounts of the events of 1821, now available online.[135] These provide abundant evidence that there were at least three hoards or stores of treasure in Lima which were taken to Callao for safety, and then either taken into the interior of Peru by Canterac, or put on the *Sacramento* (loyal to San Martin), or seized by Admiral Cochrane on behalf of the new republican government of Chile. What these witnesses have to tell us also makes it fundamentally unlikely (if not impossible) that there was a fourth hoard in Callao, which was seized by pirates.

ADMIRAL, LORD COCHRANE

The revolutions in Central and South America owed much to British support, and there were several Britons who witnessed the central events and their aftermath. By far and away the most important of these was Admiral Thomas Cochrane, 10th Earl of Dundonald (1775 – 1860), a British naval officer who had seen active service during the Napoleonic Wars. In 1818 he left the U.K. in official disgrace, as a result of his involvement in a Stock Exchange scandal; and he and his family reached Valparaiso in Chile in November 1818.

Chile was organising a navy for its war of independence; and Cochrane was appointed Vice-Admiral and took command of this force. In 1820, the rebel general Bernardo O'Higgins ordered him to convey the Liberation Army of General José de San Martín to Peru, blockade the coast, and support the campaign for independence in that region. Later, forces under Cochrane's command cut out and captured the frigate *Esmeralda*, the most powerful Spanish ship in South America. All this helped the cause of Peruvian independence, which O'Higgins considered indispensable to the security of the infant Chilean Republic; but there were many quarrels between the rebel leaders, and Cochrane was to leave the service of the Chilean Navy in November 1822, before taking command in Brazil.

---

135   James Higgins *Emancipation of Peru*, https://sites.google.com/site/jhemanperu.

Cochrane's *Narrative of Services in the Liberation of Chili, Peru and Brazil* was not published until 1859, some forty years after the event, but it represented a collection of several volumes of memoirs which must have been written long before that; and it consistently has the ring of truth.[136] Moreover, the Admiral quotes extensively from his subordinate W.B.Stevenson's *Narrative*, published in 1825.

Cochrane says nothing about pirates when he describes the plunder of Lima in 1821; and yet he had complete command of the sea, and the harbour of Callao, at the time. It is true that he does mention the presence of certain merchant vessels in the harbour, and at a critical moment; but there is nothing to suggest that any of these was British, or managed to make off with any treasure. Nor does Cochrane refer to an identifiable 'Treasure of Lima.' He does tell us, in some detail, what happened to two distinct hoards of treasure during the critical year of the Revolution; but neither of them was seized by pirates, and neither of them was taken to Cocos Island.

We will begin with Cochrane's description of the deposition of Viceroy de la Pezuela, in January 1821.

> So dissatisfied were the Spanish troops at Lima with the government of their Viceroy, Pezuela, to whose want of military capacity they absurdly attributed our successes, that they forcibly deposed him, after compelling him to appoint General Lacerna [sic] as his successor. The deposed Viceroy wishing to send his lady and family to Europe, applied to General San Martin for a passport, to avoid capture by the Chilian squadron. This was refused; but Lady Cochrane having arrived at Callao in the British frigate *Andromache*, to take leave of me previous to her departure for England, the Viceroy's lady, Donna Angela, begged of her Ladyship to use her influence with the General to obtain leave for her departure for Europe. Lady Cochrane immediately proceeded to Haura, and effected the object.

---

136 Although Andrew Lambert, in the ODNB, describes the Narrative as 'colourful, if imperfect.'

It is clear from this that the deposition of La Pezuela was made in an orderly fashion, and indeed with a high degree of courtesy. It is unlikely, therefore, that this Viceroy was involved in any underhand attempt to smuggle away any part of the wealth of Peru.

The next extract from Cochrane's *Narrative* relates to events which took place in May 1821, when there was an armistice between royalists and revolutionaries. Despite this, Cochrane continued to blockade the Peruvian coast; and he now tells us that he intercepted a ship loaded with treasure; but this is clearly not the *Mary Dear*, though a lady of a different kind was involved in the action.

> I received private information that a ship of war laden with treasure was about to make her escape in the night. There was no time to be lost, as the enemy's vessel was such an excellent sailer that, if once under weigh, beyond the reach of shot, there was no chance of capturing her. I therefore determined to attack her... Having beat to quarters, we opened fire upon the treasure-ship and other hostile vessels in the anchorage, the batteries and gun-boats returning our fire, Lady Cochrane remaining on deck during the conflict. Seeing a gunner hesitate to fire his gun, close to which she was standing, and imagining that his hesitation from her proximity might, if observed, expose him to punishment, she seized the man's arm, and directing the match fired the gun. The effort was, however, too much for her, as she immediately fainted, and was carried below.[137]

Now this incident might suggest that Lord Cochrane's blockade was not completely effective, and we are not told whether this particular vessel managed to get away in the end. However, if she was an enemy warship as described, she could not have been the brig *Mary Dear*; and, whilst it is possible that there were other vessels which managed to evade Cochrane's long arm, the possibility is not a probability.

---

137 This incident was reported in the *Caledonian Mercury* for 24 September 1821 and the *Birmingham Chronicle* for 27 September 1821.

What we do know is that the rebel advance on Lima began again; and July 1821 proved to be a momentous month in the history of the Revolution. One feature of this was the unfortunate difference of opinion which developed between the rebel leaders, which was to have serious consequences for the governance of the new republic.

> We arrived at Callao [the port of Lima] on the 2nd of July, when [we learned] that Lima was no longer tenable from want of provisions, and that an intention existed on the part of the Viceroy [de la Serna] to abandon it. On the 6th the Viceroy abandoned the city, retaining, however, the fortresses at Callao, the garrison of which was reinforced from the troops which had evacuated Lima; a large quantity of warlike stores being also deposited in the forts, thus securing greater efficiency than before.
>
> To the astonishment of the Peruvians and Chilenos, no movement was made by the liberating army [led by San Martin] to take possession of the Capital; and as the Spanish troops were withdrawn, whilst no government existed, serious disorders were anticipated, so that the *Cabildo* [Mayor] applied to Capt. Basil Hall, then in command of the British ship of war *Conway*, for his assistance to maintain tranquillity and protect public and private property. Captain Hall immediately despatched a party of marines, who contributed to maintain order.
>
> General San Martin having been apprised by the Viceroy of his intention to abandon the capital, had entered the harbour in the schooner *Sacramento*, but nevertheless gave no orders for its occupation.
>
> As the forts at Callao were still in the possession of the enemy, I made preparations to attack them, and to destroy the shipping still sheltered under them. Aware of my intentions, the garrison, on the 11th, sank the *San Sebastian*, the only frigate left in the harbour, in order to prevent her falling into our hands. On the following day, the *O'Higgins, Lautaro, Puyrredon*, and *Potrillo* arrived, so that the squadron was again complete.

On [18 July] General San Martin directed a civic guard to be organized in place of the Spanish guard which had evacuated the city, the Marquis of Torre Tagle being appointed its commandant. [But] had a division of the liberating army been sent to co-operate with the guerillas, the entire Spanish force might have been annihilated, in place of forming the *nucleus*—as they afterwards did—of a force which, after my departure from Chili, threatened not only the independence of Peru, but even that of the Chilian Republic itself.

The retreating Spaniards committed great excesses amongst the inhabitants of the interior, who found themselves exposed to more than the rigours of martial law, without the least attempt for their protection... [But] in place of protecting the Peruvians in the interior, a number of highly inflated proclamations were issued [by General San Martin], in which it was left to be inferred that the city had been taken by hard fighting, though not a blow had been struck...

On the 24th I ordered Captain Crosbie to proceed to Callao in the boats, and cut out as many of the enemy's vessels as he could bring away. The service was gallantly performed, for on the following day he brought out two large merchantmen, the *San Fernando* and *Milagro*, and the sloop of war *Resolucion*, together with several launches; burning moreover two vessels within musket shot of the batteries.

On the 27th, the *Cabildo* sent me an invitation to be present at the public proclamation of the independence of Peru... Imagining that myself and officers had been mainly instrumental in establishing the independence of Peru—for I had in vain urged the Captain-General to action, as far as the army was concerned, the invitation was accepted, but judge of my surprise at the ceremony, when medals were distributed, ascribing to General San Martin and the army the whole credit of having accomplished that which the squadron had achieved!

In August 1821, relations between Admiral and the General deteriorated still further.

> On the 3rd of August [1821], General San Martin issued a proclamation.... and declared himself 'Protector of Peru'... Being at the time on board the flag-ship, I knew nothing of this proclamation; but as the squadron had not been paid their twelve months' wages, nor the 50,000 dollars promised by General San Martin, I went on shore on the 4th of August, to make the demand on behalf of the squadron, the seamen having served their time. Being ignorant of the self-imposed title which General San Martin had assumed, I frankly asked him to devise some means for defraying these payments.

An acrimonious correspondence now took place between Cochrane and San Martin, in which the Admiral made it clear that he strongly disapproved of the General's dictatorial behaviour. In particular, he thought that San Martin had betrayed the Chilean sailors who had done so much to bring about the revolution, by refusing to pay them. San Martin's reply was to issue a proclamation, *promising* arrears of pay for the seamen, and a pension for life for the officers, but acknowledging these as officers of Peru. Cochrane thought this was an attempt to persuade his men to desert from the Chilean service especially since no arrears were in fact paid. He also tells us that, when the Archbishop of Lima made his opposition to the new Protector known, he was ordered to close all religious houses 'of spiritual exercise'. The Archbishop eventually embarked in a merchant vessel for Rio de Janeiro. Cochrane regarded this expulsion as arbitrary and foolish, and became even more concerned for the future of his own men.

> The affairs of the squadron becoming every day worse, and a mutinous spirit being excited from actual destitution, I endeavoured to obtain possession of the castles of Callao by negotiation, offering to the Spanish Commandant permission to depart with two-thirds of the property contained in the fort, on condition of the remainder,

together with the forts, being given up to the Chilian squadron. My object was to supply the crews with the absolute necessaries, of which they stood in need from the evasive conduct of the Protector...

Cochrane added the following detail, which is highly significant from our point of view:

There were large sums and a vast amount of plate in the possession of the Spanish garrison - the wealthy citizens of Lima - fearing their liberators - having deposited both in the forts for security. A third of this would have relieved us from our embarrassments.

It should be noted therefore that, in early September 1821, there was still a large amount of treasure in Callao, albeit this is said to have belonged to the inhabitants of Lima, rather than to the Peruvian government.

Cochrane tells us that his offer to the royalist commander of Callao was rejected. San Martin then accused the Admiral of wanting to seize the treasure in Callao for himself. However, a third force now intervened, in the shape of General Canterac, who was still loyal to Viceroy de la Serna, and hence to Madrid. Cochrane starts by quoting from W.B. Stevenson's work; but then adds a comment of his own.

[Stevenson] General Canterac, with 3,200 men, passed to the southward of Lima within half-musket shot of the protecting army of Peru, composed of 12,000, entered the castles of Callao with a convoy of cattle and provisions, where he refreshed and rested his troops for six days, and then retired on the 15th, taking with him the *whole of the vast treasure deposited therein by the Limeños*, and leisurely retreating on the north side of Lima." [Emphasis added].

[Cochrane] The preceding extract, published in London by one who was by my side during the whole affair, is perfectly correct. The Limeños were deeply humiliated by the occurrence, nor was their annoyance mitigated by the publication of the following proclamation in the ministerial *Gazette* of the 19th, in which General San Martin informed them that he had beaten the enemy and pursued the fugitives!¹³⁸ Though the said enemy had relieved and reinforced the fortress, and then coolly walked off unmolested with plate and money to the amount of many millions of dollars; in fact, *the whole wealth of Lima, which, as has been said, was deposited by the inhabitants in the fortress for security.*¹³⁹ [Emphasis added].

Cochrane goes on to describe subsequent events, by way of justifying his decision to seize at least some of the remaining wealth of Lima, his purpose being to pay the sailors of the Chilean Squadron, and forestall the attempt of San Martin to pay his own troops. However, it is clear that San Martin did succeed in seizing some of what had been feared lost as a result of Canterac's raid.

> Fortunately for Chili and myself, an occurrence took place which averted the evil and was brought about by the very means which the Protector had devised to promote his individual views. The occurrence alluded to was the embarcation of large sums of money by the Protector in his yacht *Sacramento*, which had cast out her ballast to stow the silver, and in a merchant vessel in the harbour, to the exclusion of the *Lautaro* frigate, then at the anchorage. This money was sent to Ancón on the pretence of placing it in safety from any attack by the Spanish forces…
>
> I determined that the squadron should be no longer starved nor defrauded. I therefore sailed to Ancón and personally seized the treasure before witnesses, respecting all that professed to belong

---

138 Cochrane invoked Shakespeare in order to describe San Martin's claim that he had scored a great victory at Callao : 'To these monstrous assertions I only know one parallel, viz:—Falstaff's version of his victory over the robbers at Gadshill'.

139 This is the passage which Hancock and Weston quote as the basis for their assertion that Cochrane noted the removal of treasure by Canterac's royalist force as taking place on August 19 1821; but in fact Cochrane does not put a date to that event – which actually took place a month later. This radically undermines their theory that Thompson had already removed a different 'treasure of Lima': H&W, Appendix I, 296.

to private individuals and also the whole of that contained in the Protector's schooner *Sacramento*, considering it his private property, though it could not have been other than plunder wrested from the Limeños. *Independently of this yachtload of silver, there were also on board seven sacks of uncoined gold brought down on his account by the legate Paroissien; so that after all the moveable wealth of Lima was supposed to have been previously deposited for safety in the castles of Callao but carried off by Cantarac, the condition of the unhappy Limeños may be imagined from the additional sums of which they were subsequently deprived.* [Emphasis added].

San Martin did not take this lying down. He made strenuous attempts to regain what Cochrane had taken; but to no avail. The argument brought an end to the alliance between the General and the Admiral, and Cochrane returned to Chile, where Brazil, Mexico and Greece were all bidding for his services. Small wonder that Cochrane helped to inspire the fiction of his one-time midshipman, Frederick Marryat and, much later, the novels of Patrick O'Brien.[140]

So there we have it. Cochrane has unwittingly solved a problem he was never set. He has shown that that there was no Treasure of Lima, but at least three separate hoards – those taken by Canterac, by San Martin and by himself; and he has done so without the benefit of piratical intervention, or the involvement of a distant desert island. Moreover, there is confirmation of the main facts in his *Narrative*, in other British sources.

THE TIMES, 1822

There are two articles in *The Times* of London which tell us that the main threat to the treasure taken to Callao for safekeeping, during the crisis of 1821, came from the revolutionary forces, rather than from any pirates who might have been lurking off the coast of Peru, or indeed from General Canterac. In March 1822 the newspaper contained a report from a Republican made on 27

---
140   Lambert in ODNB.

October 1821 'that Canterac had briefly occupied Callao but that the guerrillas [that is the rebels] had during his advance carried everything off.' The reporter continued in the same vein.

> The passengers further state that the object of General Canterac in his advance... was to obtain possession of two or more million dollars belonging chiefly to private individuals who were supposed to be shut up in the fortress... but, finding a little money, he fled.

The second item in *The Times* in August 1822 referred to a report in an American newspaper, stating that Canterac's retreat from Callao had been 'precipitate.' However one reads this, there is nothing which points the finger of suspicion at Captain Thompson.[141]

BASIL HALL, 1824

Basil Hall served as captain of H.M.S. *Conway* on the Royal Navy's Pacific Station. It was his job to keep an eye on British interests in the region, and report back. He also had an opportunity to observe and interview San Martin, and he presents a relatively sympathetic assessment of him and his career, which contrasts strongly with the opinions formed by other British writers. However, his account of Canterac's raid is the same as theirs. His *Extracts from a Journal written on the coasts of Chili, Peru and Mexico in the Years 1820, 1821 and 1822* was published in Edinburgh in 1824; and we have already seen how useful Admiral Chambers found this publication. The main point of relevance to the myth of 'the Treasure of Lima' is the following passage concerning Canterac's raid on Callao.

> It may be remembered that when we left Peru on the 10th of August General San Martin had entered Lima and declared himself Protector, but that Callao still held out and, as long as this was the case, the Independent cause remained in imminent hazard. San Martin,

---
141 *The Times*, 1 March 1822; 15 August 1822.

therefore, employed every means of intrigue to reduce the Castle, as he had no military force competent to its regular investment. It was supposed that, in process of time, he would have succeeded in starving the garrison into terms, but on the 10th of September, to the surprise of everyone, a large Spanish force from the interior marched past Lima and entered Callao. San Martín drew up his army in front of the capital as the enemy passed, but did not choose to risk an engagement. The Spaniards remained but a few days in Callao and then retired to the interior for want of provisions, *carrying off the treasure which had been deposited in the Castle*. [Emphasis added].

WILLIAM BENNET STEVENSON, 1825

Author of *A Historical and Descriptive Narrative of Twenty Years' Residence in South America*, (1825), Stevenson served as Lord Cochrane's personal secretary. His massive three-volume work covers Chile, Peru and Colombia and is motivated by a desire to give the British public an understanding of those countries and of the changes which have taken place there; but for our purposes, it is important to remind ourselves that it confirms Cochrane's account at several points. In particular it confirms the story of Canterac's successful raid on Callao, and then spells out the consequences.

> Had the force under General Cantarac been attacked, it must have been beaten… If it be asked, who is blameable for this dereliction of duty to the cause of American liberty? I must answer, San Martín! The Spaniards themselves confess that had the division under Cantarac been destroyed on the tenth of September, they should have lost all hopes of reconquering the country and should have immediately negotiated in the most honourable terms possible for themselves and abandoned America.
>
> Fearing a reverse at Lima, on the approach of the Spanish troops under General Cantarac, the treasures belonging to the government as well as the property of many individuals had been sent down to

Ancón and embarked, not on board the Chilean frigate *Lautaro*, then at anchor in that port but in several merchant vessels to prevent them falling into the hands of the enemy…

So here again there is a reference to merchant vessels, and we are told that some part of the treasure is said to have been placed on board them; but Stevenson does not say that they were British and he does not give them or their crew a name.

Stevenson's *Narrative* does not end there. He adds a fascinating detail concerning an event which occurred some months after Cochrane had broken with San Martin and sailed away from Peru altogether.

Cochrane ordered *Lautaro, Galvarino, Valparaiso, O,Higgins, Independencia, Valdivia, Auraucano,* and the prizes San Fernando and Mercedes to Guayaquil. He intended for a cruise on the coast of Mexico…

On 11 November 1821 we reached the small island of Cocos, so-called from the abundance of palms which grow there. Lord Cochrane landed, and a *felucca*[142] hove into sight. A signal was immediately made to the *Valdivia* to chase and having captured her she proved to be a deserter from Callao. The men on board informed his lordship that, after the departure of the Chilean vessels of war, San Martin objected to pay them for their arrears, even those who left the *Valdivia* at Ancón without the year's pay given to the rest, and the reward or premium promised.

The *felucca* had been manned by pressgangs in the service of Peru and sent to the *chorillos*,[143] to prevent all kinds of smuggling but she had taken up a cargo of contraband goods part of which were still on board. When the captain was on shore the crew rose and took possession of the vessel, which they named *Retaliation*; and took to the

---

142 A traditional wooden sailing boat.
143 A district of Lima.

sea. Cochrane did not feel justified in punishing these men. They were allowed to escape.

This is the only occasion when there is any reference in these contemporary British accounts of the Peruvian Revolution, to Cocos Island. It does perhaps show that the island was not impossibly distant, and that a small vessel like a brig could in theory have undertaken the journey; but that is all it shows. It provides no confirmation of any element of the traditional legend.

THE AMERICAN CITIZEN, 1826

Finally, the '*View of South America and Mexico*', by a US citizen, which we have previously referred to, is much more favourable to San Martin than many of the British sources. Yet even this confirms the success of Canterac's raid.

> On the 28th of July, 1821, the independence of Peru was solemnly proclaimed. The troops were drawn up in the great square, in the centre of which was erected a lofty stage, in front which San Martin, accompanied by the governor and some of the principal inhabitants, displayed for the first time the independent flag proclaiming that Peru was *Free* and *independent,* by the general wish of the people, and the justice of her cause: Then waving the flag, San Martin exclaimed, *Vive La Patria! Vive La Liberta! Vive La Independence!* Which was reiterated by the multitude in the square, while the bells rung a joyous peal and cannon were discharged amidst the universal acclamations of the people. On the 3d of August, San Martin took upon himself the title of protector of Peru, and issued a proclamation.
>
> This proclamation concluded by declaring that the supreme political authority and military command were united in him, under the title of protector… San Martin now proceeded steadily in recruiting and disciplining his army, in reforming the local abuses in the administration of affairs, and in preparing and organizing a provisional

government, until the permanent constitution of the state could be established…

On the 10th of September, the Spanish army returned from the interior, and marching past Lima, entered Callao. As it passed the capital, San Martin drew up his army, but did not attack the enemy, wisely foreseeing that an increase of the garrison of Callao would diminish their provisions, and hasten the surrender of the fortress. *The Spanish army, after a short stay, retired, carrying off the treasures deposited in the castle, which shortly after surrendered to the independents.*[144] [Emphasis added].

This American account makes it clear that there was more than one moment in 1821 when the more prosperous inhabitants (and institutions) of Lima had good cause to fear for their property, and might have taken steps to conceal it or, better still, have it taken to a place of safety. That said, the anonymous American seems to have been in no doubt that the 'Spanish army' which came out of the interior in September 1821, entered Callao and made off back into the interior, managed to take away a large quantity of valuable material. There is no suggestion here that these loyalists only took away only what was there, or that what they took was not the most important part; and no reason to doubt what the American says, by reference to Lord Cochrane's account or any other. At the same time, it must be admitted that a lot turns on the meaning of that single final sentence.

---

144 By 'independents' the writer meant the republicans.

Chapter 10

THE MYTH REVIVED

After the inevitable interruption of travel caused by the Second World War, the interest in treasure-hunting revived, and adventurers began to arrive on Cocos Island once more. Christopher Weston includes photographs of some of these late-comers in his book *La Isla del Coco* (1992). We can see the faces there, of Harlow P. Merrick and Senora Marina Quirinos (1948), Ian McBean (1955), Pierre Brutus (1963), Gerry Jest (1964), Wolfgang Lietz (1987), and Albert Mata (1990).[145] There were also some prominent individuals whose stories can be told in some detail.

EARL JERMYN

Hancock and Weston write of several expeditions mounted by Victor Frederick Cochrane Hervey, Earl Jermyn and 6th Marquess of Bristol (1915-1985), who was a descendant of Lord Cochrane. Although the reader will be sceptical about much of the detail, the story does confirm that British aristocrats in search of adventure were still prepared to make the journey to Cocos Island, despite two World Wars, the Wall Street Crash, the slump and the landslide election of a Labour Government in 1945. The fears of Evelyn

---

145 C. Weston, 62-3.

Waugh and Osbert Sitwell that the great days of the upper classes were over, and that the future now belonged to the Common Man, proved unfounded. At least in some cases the aristocracy was able to restore their 'stately homes' and even their way of life, and this sometimes included a taste for adventure. Earl Jermyn provides us with the classic example.

Hervey (as he seems to have been called) was educated at Eton and Sandhurst, but was expelled from the latter because of a 'bad temperament'. He became known as the 'Pink Panther' and was the ringleader of a gang of former public school boys known as the 'Mayfair Playboys'. In July 1939, he was arrested, charged with stealing jewellry, rings and a mink fur coat, with a total value of £2,500 from premises in Mayfair, and a further £2,860 of jewellry from a property on Park Lane and was sentenced to three years' imprisonment. Much later, he went to Cocos Island with his first wife, whom he married in 1959.

> One day, while rummaging among papers belonging to his ancestor, Admiral Lord Cochrane, Hervey found what looked like Captain Thompson's directions for locating the Cocos treasure. As soon as he could, he sailed for Jamaica and there organized an expedition. But young Hervey had trouble. This first came over the electronic device he had counted on to spot the gold amid Cocos' hematite sands; its inventor quarrelled with Hervey, wrecked the instrument, and flew home to England. Then the captain of the special landing craft Hervey had hired got tired of waiting and sailed off on another job. But at the Kingston yacht club, Hervey found a friend in need - blonde, fortyish Lillian Lowell Sorensen.
>
> Hervey continued his expedition aboard the 70-foot ketch *Culver*, taking along his heavy digging gear and a labor gang of *tico* beachcombers. Mrs. Sorensen was to follow with food and other supplies as soon as she could get repairs made on the *Langesund*.
>
> At Cocos, Hervey's party got down to business. Hervey was betting on Wafer Bay on the theory that in December, when his papers said Captain Thompson had put in, only Wafer Bay would have provided adequate shelter. But he never got a chance to test his theory,

for when the *Langesund* failed to arrive with food, his Costa Rican laborers mutinied. Hervey and his party returned to Puntarenas. The *Langesund,* it turned out, had been stuck with engine trouble.

The last we heard, Hervey, Earl Jermyn, and his wife, the Countess, were living in luxury on their yacht in the Thames, but we don't think he was paying the bills with Cocos gold.[146]

Marcus Scriven's study of Hervey in *Splendour and Squalor* (Atlantic Books 2009) tells us that he was 'a fantastist, a charmer, a raconteur… [and] a drunk'; and gives several examples of occasions when he is known to have lied about his alleged adventures. However, although it is fundamentally unlikely that he would have discovered anything about Thompson in Lord Cochrane's papers, it appears that he did go to Cocos Island, though he embroidered the story with some fantastic details.

In the 1950s he had led a hunt for what he said was £14 million worth of treasure on Cocos Island, in the Pacific (the expedition yielded anecdotal and photographic riches, if nothing else')…

He assured a friend, Moira Lister, that he had shot two men in a mutiny whilst treasure-hunting on Cocos Island, 360 miles off the coast of Costa Rica. According to one of John's friends, the claim might have been uncharacteristically modest. 'We found a packet of photographs', he remembers. 'One of them showed Victor standing with his foot on four dead bodies.' He had, he assured Moira Lister years later, retrieved $1 million before a mutiny erupted, but had yet to return for the rest.[147]

HANCOCK & WESTON, 1960
In 1960 Ralph Hancock and Julian Weston's book was published in the USA. Hancock was an American writer and journalist specialising in Latin

---
146 H&W, 292-3.
147 Scriven, 67-8, 114, 361(n 66).

American affairs, while Weston was a British journalist who lived for many years in Central America, was friendly with 'succeeding political regimes in Costa Rica' and collected a large amount of 'data, original documents, maps, clippings, letters, photographs and personal narratives', relating to Cocos Island. On Weston's death in 1956, this collection was given to Hancock by Weston's heirs. Meanwhile, Hancock had himself added the fruit of his own research, in American newspapers and magazines.[148]

The book, published in the U.S.A. in 1960, is a very useful starting point for the study of the Cocos Island treasure; and must have given a considerable boost to treasure-hunting in the Americas; but it is short on verifiable facts and long on semi-fictional narrative. Like Montmorency before them, the authors do not hesitate to embroider the story with apparently convincing details and dialogue, for which they have no evidence at all. At one point, they say this.

> As far as existing documents can be relied upon, the Lima treasure is a historical treasure, by which we mean that it existed at one time. Furthermore, the available evidence indicates that the Lima treasure was buried on Cocos Island, and, so far as we can determine, it has never come to light.[149]

This is merely parroting what was said forty years before, in the Peace Handbook. What are these 'existing documents' which are referred to? Hancock & Weston do not tell us:

> We shall have to vouch for its authenticity, since the actual records cannot be offered in proof because they constitute perhaps the most valuable possession in our files. Take our word for it, this information, heretofore undisclosed, came into our hands labelled "authentic". We have checked it in every possible way and find it reliable,

---

148 H&W, 8-9. H&W do not refer to British newspaper clippings. I have searched the British Newspaper Archive in vain for relevant references to the Treasure of Lima, William Thompson and the *Mary Dear* in the early years ie 1800-1849 (see final chapter).
149 H&W, 16.

unadulterated, virgin material, of which not a word has been altered since it was first written down over a hundred years ago.'

What sort of argument is this? Why should we accept a piece of evidence as authentic, just because it is labelled as such? And why should we accept that it need not be disclosed, just because it is valuable?

Hancock & Weston say they have searched Admiralty records but found no trace of the *Mary Dear*, but do not tell us which records. They say they have checked all other records in every possible way, but again give no details. They claim to have looked 'in old churches and British shipping files' (and found nothing), but fail to specify which.[150] They give no references to any primary sources which show that Captain Thompson was able to seize the so-called Treasure of Lima in the 1820s and, when discussing how Thompson passed his secret on to Keating, they readily admit that 'we have been unable to uncover a single scrap of evidence on which these stories could have been based.'

In fact Hancock & Weston only have two pieces of evidence for the existence of the Treasure of Lima and its transportation to Cocos Island. The first is an extract from Admiral Cochrane's 'Diary', and the second is the account of the anonymous American Citizen, both of which have been considered above. In each case, their quotations are selective and highly misleading; and yet they could have got the detail right, since both books had been published many years previously.

To be fair to them, Hancock & Weston did propose a radical reinterpretation. They suggested that it was the first mate of the *Mary Dear* who had the idea of seizing the Treasure of Lima, once it had been entrusted to Captain Thompson by the Viceroy; that he instigated a mutiny for the purpose, and then gave Thompson the choice of joining the enterprise, or death. Supposedly, Thompson joined in under duress, but played a subordinate part in the affair thereafter. Hancock & Weston even named the first mate, whom they described as a 'young Scotch doctor'. Supposedly, he was

---

150   H&W, 30.

James Alexander Forbes I, who eventually passed the secret on to his son and grandson.

The central piece or pieces of evidence for this theory – 'the most valuable possession in [Hancock & Weston's files' – was

> a chart and several documents, all in [J.A.Forbes I's] handwriting, which was a map of Cocos Island, of Chatham Bay to be precise… describing in detail how the *Mary Dear*'s treasure was buried on the island and [giving] full instructions for finding it.[151]

Disappointingly, this is among the documentation which the writers decline to show us. We are asked to take it on trust.

Suppose they were right. All this would show is that it was the first mate, rather than Captain Thompson, who first set the hare running, by claiming that a hoard of treasure was taken on board the *Mary Dear* and was subsequently hidden on Cocos Island. However, the same authors provide us with several good reasons for disbelieving their theory. They point out, for example, that there are numerous stories about the burial of treasure on Cocos Island, but all have an uncanny similarity.

> Almost every story of the finding of the Cocos Island treasure, from the time of Keating and Bogue in 1846 right down to Bergmans and Bellamy almost a hundred years later, has a common central theme and it is only in the minor details that there is any variation.

The story always tells how two men visited Cocos Island, stumbled across the treasure in a cave; how one of the two men died, either before or after leaving the island; how the survivor eventually managed to get back to civilization, taking with him a "small portion" of the treasure to "prove" his story; and how he spent the rest of his life trying to get back to the island, whether by

---

151 H&W, 274.

himself or by persuading a rich backer to fit out an expedition.¹⁵² Well, yes, but what are we supposed to infer from this?

In conclusion, Hancock & Weston did a great deal to undermine the foundations of the traditional British version of the myth; but they still believed that the Treasure of Lima was 'an historical treasure'. At the same time, they tried to alter the myth fundamentally, not by removing Thompson from the picture altogether, but by making him change places with his first mate, rather as if someone were to switch Othello and Iago around in Shakespeare's play. By identifying the mate as James Alexander Forbes I, they were able to draw on the materials allegedly preserved by James Alexander Forbes II, and ultimately bequeathed to the treasure-hunter James Alexander Forbes IV, who (as we have seen) had organized several expeditions to Cocos Island. This suited their purpose, because their book was published in New York; and whereas Thompson had been British, the Forbes dynasty was American, and an important family to boot. Moreover, their book was published in 1960, when the Americans had become rather famous for claiming every success as their own.

ROBERT VERGNES, 1962-78

Robert Vergnes (1927-2004) was a speleologist, explorer and treasure-seeker but, above all, a professional adventurer. Eventually, he attempted to earn his living by writing; but he remained a man of action, rather than one of letters. He was not concerned with evidence, but with intuition and imagination, which he thought more important than knowledge (*"L'imagination est plus importante que le savoir"*). His narratives only come alive when he is involved; and even then, we may wonder whether he is telling us the unvarnished truth.

Vergnes was the author of several books, including *L'Or dans la Peau* (1974) and *La Dernière Île Au Trésor* (1978, 2014), both of which tell the story of his first and most exciting expedition to Cocos Island in 1962. He can also be seen in a 48 minute video on YouTube entitled *Les Français du bout du monde* (2012), which again focuses on that first and fateful treasure-hunt.

---

152 H&W, 46-7.

The film (which was produced after his death) also shows him at the end of his life, when he evidently took pleasure in drink, cigars, roulette and the company of women, in the bars and clubs of Central America. By this stage he had evidently decided that the most fabulous of all treasures is life itself (*Le plus fabuleux des trésors, c'est la vie.*)[153]

Like many of the treasure seekers who wrote about their expeditions afterwards, Vergnes was only too ready to accept what people told him. So he did not question the traditional stories handed down by the British sources about Thompson and the *Mary Dear*; but he also believed in the American tradition starting with Thompson's first-mate, as well as the stories accepted by Gissler about Manoel Cabral and 'Old Mac'. Despite the many discrepancies between these three accounts, Vergnes was not prone to doubt. In his first book about Cocos Island he accepted that it was 'Captain Shrapnel' of HMS *Haughty* who landed on the Island in 1896, though (as we have seen) these were fairly obvious pseudonyms.[154]

Likewise, Vergnes bought the idea that a real 'clue' to the whereabouts of the treasure had been acquired by a French sea-captain called Tony Mangel in Sydney in 1929. Supposedly Mangel had come into the possession of documents which had once belonged to Thompson and had subsequently been passed to 'Fitzgerald'. Mangel had also (supposedly) seen a letter, written by Fitzgerald, in the Nautical Club of Sydney and had even discovered an inventory of the treasure prepared by Thompson himself, in the museum of Caracas.[155] This included

> A Virgin 2 metres tall, made of gold, with the Infant Jesus, with its crown and its chest of 780 pounds, wrapped in a gold chasuble, with 1,684 stones including 3 four-inch emeralds on its chest and 6 six-inch topazes on the crown; 7 diamond crosses.[156]

---

153 Vergnes (1974) 201.
154 Vergnes did realise this by the time he wrote his second book on the subject: Vergnes (1978) 129.
155 Vernes (1974) 143-4. The list is also reproduced in Vergnes (1978), 62-3.
156 Vergnes, 144.

Although Vergnes became 'greener' as he grew older, he believed in the existence of the treasure to his dying day. Because of the strength of this faith, he was able to dismiss any doubts arising from the fact more than one of the maps and documents which he acquired were obvious forgeries. (One map showing where Thompson and his mate had buried the loot was dated 1820, a whole year before they were supposed to have seized the Treasure of Lima).[157] He convinced himself that the only reason previous adventurers had failed was because of 'bad luck, erroneous clues, poor interpretation of maps, the changing nature of the physical geography on the island, lack of time and shortage of the right equipment.' He thought that more research was needed.[158]

Vergnes made four expeditions to the Island in 1962, '73, '76 and' 78; but it is the first of these which was crucial. The background was that in 1957 he learned of the existence of Cocos Island from a journalist in Costa Rica, who told him that it was home to a fabulous treasure which had been accumulated by the notorious pirate Captain Henry Morgan (c1635-1688)! Then he met Jean Portelle and Claude Chaliès in Paris, and the three men made a plan, which included, from the outset, the idea of writing a book and making a film about their adventure.

Vergnes said that they reached the Island late in 1962, were set down and then loaded – or rather overloaded – a dinghy, and set off for the shore; but the dinghy capsized, and all three were thrown into the sea. Vergnes made it to the shore but Portelle could not swim, he said, and had dragged Challiés down with him. Vergnes concluded that they had both drowned. He then spent two months alone on the Island before he was rescued. The journal which he somehow managed to keep at the time describes how he spent his time bemoaning his fate, but also scavenging for food, exploring the interior of the island (despite its impenetrability) and playing *petanque* with rocks found on the beach, which he somehow managed to paint red and green. He

---

157 Vergnes (1978), photos following page 192.
158 Vergnes (1978), 163.

also discovered evidence of previous French expeditions to the Island in the form of graffiti drawn on the rocks.[159]

Despite the torments he went through Vergnes also found the time and the energy to do a little treasure-hunting. On 14 February 1963 he rowed from Chatham Bay towards 'the Bay of Hope' (*Bahia de Esperanza*), which had actually been renamed Yglesias Bay in the time of President Yglesias (1894-1902).[160] This was an extraordinary journey to make single-handed, in a small open boat; but he said he had little or no difficulty.[161]

Once in the Bay, he found the entrance to a creek and a large sea-cave, two metres above the level of high tides. At the far end there was a place where the cave divided into two, but both passages were blocked, and it seemed to Vergnes that the blockage was man-made. He asked himself 'Is this Thompson's cave'? Then he discovered a second cave nearby, only accessible at low tide, from which it was possible to reach a small platform, which provided an entrance to the first. He became really excited; but had to leave almost immediately because of the rising tide; and, when he came back the following day, the weather had turned against him, and he found it impossible to land, or find the cave again.[162]

Vergnes was not easily put off. He returned to Cocos Island in 1973 on a 13 metre French yacht, the *Almaria II*, with a small crew of amateurs, who were not even good sailors, let alone explorers. It was agreed that, on arrival on the Island, their first 'port' of call would again be the Bay of Hope, where he hoped to find HIS CAVE (*MA GROTTE*); but when they got there, they found that the tide was so high that they could not see it at all – it must have been under 3 or 4 metres of water, he thought. Vergnes was bitterly disappointed, re-naming it 'the Bay of Disappointment.'

On his third expedition in 1976 Vergnes discovered a large bottle with a message in it.

---

159 The visit of the French frigate *La Génie* in 1847 [sic] is mentioned in the H.M.S.O. Handbook, 22.
160 C. Weston, 108.
161 Vergnes (1978), 278.
162 Vergnes (1978), 257-9.

ISLE ¤ QUEST

GREETINGS YE FOOLS WHO SEEK THE LOOT OF LIMA.
LOOK YE NO MORE THAN THIS JUG
FOR ALL YE WILL FIND ARE ACHEING BONES TO LUG.
SEARCH IF YE MAY ONLY IN YOUR DISMAY,
TO FIND OUR FOOT PRINTS LEAD THE WAY
TO EMPTY HOLES AND CAVES, SO LADS NAY
– TAKE YE HEED OF OUR ADVICE, CHANGE
YOUR COURSE TO LIMA CITY,
FOR THEREIN UPON AN ALTAR HIGH
SMILES THE VIRGIN MARY. AYE!
SOLID GOLD SHE STANDS, SERENE AND PEACEFUL, SHE
BEMUSES WHAT FOOLS BE YOU WHO SEEK MY IMAGE
– SEARCH NOT THE COCOS JUNGLE WITH GLEE,
BUT IN YOUR BLACK HEART LIES THE KEY.
HOIST ANCHOR AND SET SAIL, IT TELLS ME,
FOR A LARGE RAINBOW AWAITS ME.
HOMEWARD BOUND IT DIRECTS THY HELM FOR THOSE
WHO CAN NOW SAY "WE HAVE TRIED ONLY TO FAIL
RATHER THAN FAIL BY NOT TO TRY."

6 FEBRUARY 1968.   SWIFT OF IPSWICH.[163]

In 1985 Peter Disch-Lauxmann gave a very different, and much more dramatic, account of Robert Vergnes's first expedition in 1962. He related that, around the same time, there was a French expedition in which Jacques Boucaud took part. This was well-prepared; but it was illegal, because those in charge had no permit from the Costa Rican government. Nevertheless, the adventurers soon had considerable success. In a hollow in the interior of the island, they found two human skeletons, and two half-rotten chests, containing a compass, a revolver and a Bible, but also a leather bag or sack, containing

---

163   Vergnes (1978), photo opposite page 193.

around 1,000 gold coins, and a shirt in which several gold bars were wrapped. The other chest also contained assorted treasures. The French then buried the two skeletons and retrieved the treasure, which they kept.

When he was first told this tale, Disch-Lauxmann was sceptical; but then he found out that Vergnes was on the Island at about the same time as Boucaud. He continues by telling us that, although Vergnes claimed that his two French companions had disappeared and were presumed drowned, Challiés's widow refused to accept this. She insisted that both her husband and his friend had been excellent swimmers; and she wanted a proper investigation. A police enquiry was duly held and, when Vergnes eventually returned to France, he was questioned about the affair; but no-one was ever able to prove anything against him.[164]

What Disch-Lauxmann tells us next makes all other accounts seem mundane. He met an old (and anonymous) American sea-captain and yachtsman who had spent many years in Costa Rica and claimed to have been to Cocos Island on more than fifteen occasions, with various expeditions. He got to know this old salt well and they began to drink together on a regular basis. The German eventually asked the American to tell what he knew about the expeditions of Boucaud and Vergnes in 1962.

One drink-fuelled evening, the American dropped the bombshell. He said the two expeditions had been one and the same! He named no names, and did not claim to have been an eye witness; but said that, to the best of his belief, the French expedition had discovered a hoard of treasure which the pirate Edward Davis had deposited on the Island towards the end of the 17th century; and the leader of it had then *murdered* his two companions, in order to keep the loot for himself. The murderer had then escaped from the Island with most of the Davis treasure, and returned home safely to Europe, where he now lived in luxury, in a villa overlooking the Mediterranean. Disch-Lauxmann remained dubious, as well he might; but, by way of 'proof', the American produced a cigarette case full of gold coins (*Rands* in German) on which the German could make out the dates 1621 and 1627.[165]

---

164 D-L, 208-212.
165 D-L, 212-221.

These are sensational stories, though no wilder than some of those told about Captain Thompson and John Keating; but it is interesting to compare what Disch-Lauxmann tells us about the French expedition(s)of 1962 with what Rollo Gebhard has to says about another such expedition, said to have been undertaken only four years later.

ROLLO GEBHARD, 1975

Rollo Gebhard.(1921 – 2013) was a German yachtsman who sailed round the world single handed on two occasions, the second voyage on the *Solveig III* starting in 1975 with a brief visit to Cocos Isand. In his book *Ein Mann und Sein Boot* (1980) he narrates the legend of the Treasure of Lima, telling us that 'Jack' Thompson was both a 'trustworthy Scotsman' and a 'good Catholic' and that the Treasure was worth some 250 million Marks and included a Madonna which weighed over a tonne. It is also remarkable that, in Gebhard's book, the search for the treasure began in 1846, with Keating, but there is no room here for Fitzgerald, let alone for James Alexander Forbes or any of Gissler's informants.

On reading about Graf Luckner's experiences in the 1930s, Gebhard wrote: 'At this point, one might think that the search was hopeless and the whole story was untrue', but concluded that 'the facts suggest that the treasure can still be found.' Having said that, he had no interest in looking for it himself: he merely wanted to 'to build up a picture of 'where the treasure might lie, and whether it might be possible to find it' by means of photography. He was particularly interested in the location of caves, in particular one cave where he understood that a French expedition had recently found two human skeletons.

Gebhard landed once or twice and explored the interior for a while. One gets the impression that he was struck by the contrast between the beauty of the natural environment and the ugliness of what the treasure seekers had left behind, in the form of rusting machinery, bits of boring and earth-moving equipment which had been left to rust, on the beaches or in the jungle nearby. It comes as no surprise to learn that, later in life Gebhard founded the *Society for Dolphin Conservation*. He was therefore a prophet of the green movement which was to transform the face of the Island some years later.

Nevertheless Gebhard cannot resist telling us the following tale, with its echoes of Vergnes and the French expedition of 1962.

> In the autumn of 1966 four young Frenchmen were set down on Cocos Island and began a systematic search which, as it happened, was a partial success. In a cave, they found the bodies of two men who had killed each other. This must have happened a hundred years previously, because the Bible, which was found among the skeletons, had been printed in Boston in 1846. When they moved one of the skeletons, the students found a knife embedded in it, which had come from a sheath worn by the other skeleton, while this second skeleton had a wound in the skull which had been inflicted with an axe, which lay next to the first skeleton. It was clear that a terrible fight had taken place between the two men.
>
> In a sack the French, who were now really alarmed by what they had found, discovered around 1,000 old gold coins and 15 bars of gold, each weighing half a pound, and finally a second sack of containing the same items. They managed to hide the coins and bars in oxygen cylinders bottles until they had brought the spoils home to France, where they paid whatever import duties were due, and they divided up what was left.

This account differs in several important respects from that given by Disch-Lauxmann. The dates of the discovery do not match; but, more importantly the presumed date of the murder (or murders) is in the 1840s, not the 1960s. The finger of suspicion does not, therefore, point in the direction of the late Robert Vergnes; but the lesson here is really that one should not place too much reliance on stories told by sailors in bars; and that note of caution might well be sounded in relation to many other stories told about the Treasure of Lima.

GERALD KINGSLAND, 1978

Gerald Kingsland (1930 – 2000) was a journalist and adventurer, who was married five times, and had five sons and two daughters. After a stint in the British Army during the Korean War, he became a wine grower in Italy. In 1980, he set out to find a remote tropical island where he could share 'the Good Life' with a female companion. Accordingly, he advertised for someone suitable in *Time Out*, using the notorious line 'writer seeks wife for a year'.

This led to his meeting Lucy Irvine, who was 24; and they went to Tuin Island, in the Torres Strait, between Australia and Papua New Guinea, where they nearly died. Nevertheless they each wrote an account of the adventure: Irvine's *Castaway* was published in 1983, Kingsland's *The Islander* in 1984. The story was also depicted in the film *Castaway*, in which Kingsland had the misfortune to be played by Oliver Reed (1938-1999), one of the more notorious 'roaring boys' of the acting profession.

This much is well-known. What few people know is that, previously, in 1978, Kingsland had taken another young woman with him to Cocos Island, where they spent 10 months. *The Times* described him as a mere 'caddish adventurer'.[166] What his true motives were remains obscure.

JACK FITZGERALD, 2005

Jack Fitzgerald is the author of *Treasure Island Revisited* (2005). He was a journalist in Newfoundland who become fascinated by the part which his fellow countryman John Keating had played in the history of treasure-hunting on Cocos Island, and also (like Ina Knobloch, with whom he collaborated in the making of a documentary) by the possible connection between Cocos Island and Robert Louis Stevenson's *Treasure Island*. As one might expect, Fitzgerald is at his best when writing about Keating; but that is not to say that we need believe in Keating's own narrative. Fitzgerald believes it all, but does not produce any evidence to show that there ever was a Captain Thompson, or a *Mary Dear*. All he says is that it is possible to piece together the story of what happened in 1821 and immediately afterwards, from primary sources.

---

166 *The Times*, 3 December, 1994.

Fitzgerald claims to be the first to have researched extensively in the genealogical records of Newfoundland, and – more importantly – in Lloyds of London's Shipping Movements for the period 1821-24;[167] but, when we actually examines the extracts he reproduces from Lloyds Shipping Registers, what we find is five ships called the *Devonshire*, and none called the *Mary Dear*.

Fitzgerald then informs us that we should not expect the name of a pirate ship to appear in an official record; and that in his view the name of the *Mary Dear* must have been changed to the *Devonshire*, in order to disguise her piratical activity. Elsewhere he tells us that he found records of two Treasures of Lima, and two Captain Thompsons; but he also tells us that Keating's Captain Thompson was called Marion, though neither of the recorded Thompsons were called that.[168] It appears that all the painstaking study of the records of Lloyds of London does not advance his case for the truth of the British tradition at all.

Fitzgerald is aware that there are sceptics: he refers to E.R. Snow's book, which regarded the Treasure of Lima as a myth; but he remains a believer; and to bolster his case, he prays in aid both Montmorency's *On the Track of a Treasure*, and Cochrane's *Narratives*. Both of these have been considered above: suffice to say that Montmorency's narrative of the events of 1821 is largely fiction; and that Cochrane's provides no support for Fitzgerald's argument.

There is one further point to make against Fitzgerald, which goes to accuracy and credibility. At page 17 he says that Cochrane met a pirate on Cocos Island on 22 December 1822, and that this was possibly Captain Marion Thompson! However, this statement must be based on W.B. Stevenson's *Historical Narrative*, and specifically his account of Cochrane's landing on Cocos in November 1821; and we have already seen how the pirates the Admiral found there on that occasion were Spaniards, on board a *felucca* which they had re-named the *Resolution*. It is inconceivable that Lord

---

167 In the Maritime History Archives of the Memorial University of St John's, Newfoundland.
168 Fitzgerald, 153, 126. He also tells us that he thinks that a William Thompson, shown in the records, was not the same man as Marion Thompson; but did go looking for him: ibid. 135, 137, 152.

Cochrane would have failed to recognise a British merchant Captain, or be mistaken as to the type of ship he was in charge of, or would have failed to take action against British pirates, if he had found any on the high seas. As it was, he let those on board the *felucca* go, because he sympathised with what they had done, which was to rebel against his erstwhile, but estranged, companion in arms, San Martin.

None of the post-War adventurers ever found anything, any more than their predecessors had; and we may ask, at this point, why none of them ever drew the obvious conclusión, the conclusión which Admiral Chambers had reached in 1935, that there was nothing awaiting discovery. Two reasons suggest themselves: first, many more people continued to read Stevenson's *Treasure Island* than ever read *Chambers's Journal* (which in any event ceased publication in 1956); and second, the spirit of adventure is more powerful, especially amongst the young, than is the critical faculty.

Chapter 11

THE GREENING OF THE ISLAND

We have seen how technology made it progressively easier for adventurers of all kinds to travel to Cocos Island, and carry out their investigations and excavations once there; but, although modern science continued to be applied after the Second World War, no treasure was ever discovered. However, there were many who remained undaunted and, even now, there are those who would go there and dig, if this were allowed. They believe that their predecessors have failed because they had insufficient or inadequate equipment, or because they looked in the wrong place. They tell themselves that, if only they could deploy the latest techniques in prospecting, the hoard would surely be found. The possibility that the Treasure of Lima, and other treasures, may not be there at all, does not seem to trouble them.

And yet, the *Zeitgeist* has changed. For many the impulse to dig for buried treasure, at the expense of the environment, has become passé, along with imperialism and colonialism. It has been replaced by a widespread desire to preserve these remote havens, along with the world's vanishing species.

Even in the 19th century, there were those who stopped off at Cocos Island for reasons unconnected with buried treasure. Scientific research, of one kind or another, was a powerful motive. We have already noted the visit paid by Sir Edward Belcher in 1838 on board H.M.S. *Sulphur*. He surveyed the island; and we know the Englishman George W. Barclay also collected plant specimens. Between 1888 and 1891, the marine zoologist and oceanographer Alexander Agassiz visited Cocos Island on his way to the Galapagos. In 1898, the government of President Yglesias sponsored the first Costa Rican expedition; and the serious study of the Island's flora and fauna has continued ever since.[169]

The first diving expedition to the Island took place in February 1905 (only a month after Earl Fitzwilliam's party had departed). The government of Costa Rica commissioned a small group of 'hard-hat' divers to explore the ocean floor which surrounds it, principally to look at the fauna. The technology was primitive by modern standards – the divers obtained their air from a manual pump on the surface. Unfortunately, no record survives of their findings, apart from a few sketches.[170] In 1925 the American naturalist and marine biologist William Beebe (1877-1962) visited the Island and recorded what he found in *The Arcturus Adventure*, though he is better known for his deep dives in the Bathysphere, However, it was only in the late 20th century that Cocos Island really began to be appreciated for its natural wonders. This followed, in particular, the Costa Rican decrees that the Island was a National Park in 1978 and the complete ban on treasure-hunting in 1994. Further, the National Park was designated a World Heritage Site by UNESCO in 1997; and in 2002, this designation was extended to include a marine zone of 771 square miles. The change of status went in hand in hand with a change of sensibility, whereby the Island ceased to be seen as fair game for plunderers masquerading as adventurers from the four corners of the Earth, and came to be regarded as a priceless asset. Certain prominent

---

169   *The orchid flora of Cocos Island National Park, Puntarenas, Costa Rica*, Diego Bogarin, Jorge Warner, Martyn Powell, and Vincent Savolainen; Botanical Journal of the Linnean Society 166(1):20-39 · May 2011.
170   C.Weston, 256-7, including illustrations.

individuals played an important part in this transformation, though it was gradual, and never entirely complete.[171]

HANS HASS

Hans Hass (1919 – 2013) was an Austrian biologist and underwater diving pioneer; and was among the first scientists to popularise coral reefs, stingrays and sharks. In the 1950s he made many films with his wife Lotte, which were shown on children's TV in the the UK; and he was a pioneer of submarine photography. In 1951 he founded the International Institute for Submarine Research and purchased the ship *Xarifa*, from which he shot the Oscar winning feature film *Unternehmen Xarifa* ('Under the Caribbean'), which included the first underwater shots of a sperm whale. Cocos Island was amongst the many places where he shot film of the abundant sealife to be found in the word's Oceans, before the advent of super-trawlers and overfishing.

JACQUES COUSTEAU

The second great 'green' pioneer was Jacques Cousteau (1910-1997), who was attracted to Cocos Island by its (then) abundant populations of hammerhead sharks, rays, dolphins and other large marine species. He visited the island several times, calling it "the most beautiful island in the world". His son Philippe-Pierre Cousteau (1940 – 1979) was also a sailor, director and cinematographer, as well as being a diver. He was the leading cameraman for most of the Cousteau films made during his lifetime, and won many awards

DISCH-LAUXMANN, 1980-85

Peter Disch-Lauxmann & Christian Pfannenschmidt's book, *Die authentische Geschichte von Stevensons 'Schatzinsel'*, published in 1985, made a large claim,

---

171 For an example of a very traditional approach, see the film shown on BBC 2's *Wideworld* in 1988 This was made by the late actress Moira Lister (1923-2007). It received a very poor review in *The Times*.

since the title means 'the authentic history of Stevenson's "Treasure Island"'; but in fact it made no real attempt to prove that Stevenson based his adventure story on Cocos Island. Otherwise, the book is remarkable only for its lack of rigour, considering that the authors were both professional journalists, and came from the country which gave birth to modern source-based history in the time of Leopold von Ranke (1795-1886). The text lacks any bibliography, footnotes or other references, but does include many passages of invented dialogue, a technique pioneered (so far as Cocos Island is concerned) by Hervey de Montmorency and Sir Malcolm Campbell.

Disch-Lauxmann seems to have been the principal writer involved; and he did visit the Island five times between 1980 and 1985. As a friend of Dr Richard Gissler, a descendant of August Gissler, he had access to some of the latter's papers. He was also able to speak to some of the adventurers who had been to Cocos in recent decades, before treasure-hunting became illegal. It should also be said that he fished in the sea, swam in the streams and ponds and took many superb colour photographs, some of which are reproduced in the book and give the reader a real 'feel' for its luxuriant vegetation, and intimidating atmosphere.

However, when it comes to the history, Disch-Lauxmann simply tells us the same old stories, as if they were established fact. So, the treasure may have been buried by one or more of three pirates: (1) Edward Davis of the *Bachelor's Delight* in the 1680s; (2) Benito Bonito around 1818-20, and (3) a Scottish Captain called *James* (not William, nor 'Bugs', nor Marion) Thompson of the *Mary Dear* of Bristol, in 1821, after he had disobeyed the orders of 'the Viceroy'.[172]

Disch-Lauxmann does refer to what he calls 'Cocos-Syndrome', by which he appears to mean the same as his disciple Ina Knobloch means, when she refers to 'treasure-fever'. In other words he does recognise the possibility that the whole idea of there being buried treasure in that particular place could be a figment of the imagination, though he clearly thinks, or believes, that there is more to it than that.

---

172 The reference to the Viceroy is at page 54 of D-L's book.

When it comes to evidence that Davis and Bonito ever amassed hoards of treasure on Cocos Island, Disch-Lauxmann is evidently content to rely on the old legal principle of *res ipsa loquitur* (the thing speaks for itself), since all he tells us is that the two pirates in question each raided up and down the coasts of the Spanish Empire in South and Central America and that the Island was a convenient base for them. This is hardly the sort of evidence which would be acceptable in a court of law. When it comes to Thompson and the Treasure of Lima, Disch-Lauxmann produces no evidence for making him a suspect, other than the same short (and misleading) extract from Lord Cochrane's 'Diary' which had been cited by Hancock & Weston twenty-five years previously.[173]

Disch-Lauxmann tell us about Thompson, and Keating, but not the shadowy Fitzgerald. Rather, the secret is passed to the Hacketts, and in particular Fred Hackett, who sailed to Cocos Island in 1897 with Keating's widow and encountered August Gissler there. The account of Gissler's long association with the Island which follows adds nothing to the very detailed account given by Hancock & Weston; but his account of a subsequent German voyage in the 1930s is of some interest. It has long been known that Dr Hubert Mazenick became interested in the lost treasure; and proposed a somewhat unusual method of discovering its precise whereabouts. The *Belfast News-Letter* for 12 September 1935 had run the following story:

PIRATES £300,000,000 TREASURE
'GHOST' EXPLAINS WHERE TO FIND IT
GERMAN ON THE HUNT

PARIS, WEDNESDAY

Hope of finding the £300,000,000 "Treasure of the Incas"[174] on Cocos Island, with the aid of a girl spiritualist medium, is sending Hubert

---

173 See chapter 9 above..
174 Note that the writer has confused the Treasure of Lima and the Treasure of the Incas, two entirely separate myths.

Mazenick, a German yachtsman, on a 5,000 miles cruise across the Atlantic on a 34-toot sailing vessel. Mazenick declared on his arrival here from Berlin that he was ready to start from Havre shortly, taking with him Margo Schneider, a dark-hailed German girl, who brought him in touch with the shade of bold, bad pirate long ago.

Beyoo Benita [sic][175] was the pirate's name. Margot saw his spirit one evening, explained Dr Mazenick. He came alone in his finest pirate costume, spoke to us for long time, and begged us to go and dig the treasure hidden by him during his adventurous existence. 'There are four dumps,' he said, representing about £300,000,000 sterling, 'Dig them up, and with all this money you shall repair the harm I did during life.'

The pirate shade then gave precise instructions about where the treasure was hidden.

"We shall go straight to the place, I shall say, 'There it is,' and the £300,000,000 will be ours" declared Mazenick.

He added that he had made an agreement with the Costa Rica Government to give them one-third of all he found in return for warship protection. The rest of the proceeds will be parcelled out among the great Powers of Europe to found charitable institutions in accordance with the wish of the pirate's ghost.

Disch-Lauxmann tells us more.

For another Cocos Island traveller, the German Margo Schneider, there was no rescue. She travelled there in the 1930s as a Medium, who pretended to be in contact with the Pirate Benito Bonito. A German yachtsman, Dr. Hubert Mazenick, had engaged Margo to go with him. She was supposed to steer him to the treasure by means of a link she had to the ghost of a pirate; but this magical and mystical method of treasure-seeking did not work; and the Medium drew a

---

175   This seems like a variation on Benito Bonito, but it is not clear whose version is the more correct, or the less false.

blank. Supposedly Mazenick became so furious because of this that he killed Margo Schneider and hid the body in the East of Wafer Bay. Whether this conjecture corresponds with the truth or not, what is certain is that Margo Schneider was never seen again.[176]

This was not the only time a medium played a part in the saga of the Cocos Island treasure or treasures. After his return from the Island, Sir Malcolm Campbell had shown a ring and a spade he had found there to a Mrs Pollock. She told him that she was sure that there were people living on the Island when he visited him, who could see him, though he never saw them. Campbell assumed that these people were a lost tribe of Incas.

Disch-Lauxmann brings his narrative down to his own day. He tells us that the number of expeditions only multiplied with the advent of modern communications and travel; and that there were all kinds of adventurers anxious to try their luck.

> Then the yacht of an English adventurer sank in a storm in Wafer Bay ...; and then in 1978 a Costa Rican ranger found a crashed US air force bomber, missing since 1943, in the middle of the jungle. A highly-indebted American was caught by the police when he tried to go looking for treasure in a stolen luxury yacht to look for treasure. The German Rollo Gebhard stopped off here, when he was making his second single-handed voyage around the world in 1975.[177]

Disch-Lauxmann tells us about an expedition which he saw setting off from Puntarenas.

> [This] was mounted by a group of adventurers from Munich and the hang-glider Reinhold Ostler, whom I and four friends met at the beginning of 1982, shortly before crossing to Cocos Island. Ostler wanted to shoot a film, but he also wanted – perhaps more than

---

176 D-L, 175.
177 D-L, 202.

anything – to look for treasure. The preparations, which took several months, were very expensive: the equipment alone cost 50,000 Marks...

When we saw the expedition again at the pier of Puntarenas at the beginning of March, they were all burnt deep brown, and a few pounds lighter, but they had gained a wealth of experience. With their detectors, they had actually located metal in two places; but, in order to dig deep enough, they would have needed to move tons of rock, and they lacked the necessary equipment. Reinhold Ostler had, however, already become a victim of Cocos-Syndrome. He would return to Cocos Island, he assured me, since he was sure that he had found treasure.

Disch-Lauxmann is a great advocate of scientific method, (at least when it comes to technology rather than historical investigation) and contemptuous of the methods employed in earlier times. So, we now have light aircraft and helicopters, and a device which can detect precious metal at a depth of 183 metres. Compare these to 'spades, treasure-charts, dynamite and the employment of mediums, who try to make contact with long dead pirates!' He even makes the scientist's eternal complaint – 'we need more research/we need more funding'; and the reason is clear.

Cocos Island is full of treasure, I am perfectly sure of it. And I also know this: I will keep looking.[178]

Disch-Lauxmann's final conclusions are bizarre. At one point he tells us that there are only two possibilities:

Either most has already been found, and has been silently and secretly taken away for reasons of security, and perhaps of dishonour. Or vast treasures still await discovery there, but not in the places indicated on treasure-maps. Cocos Island is volcanic; and you must reckon

---

178 D-L, 225.

about 100 minor earthquakes there every year, the product of the "Cocos-Ridge," which is some 4,000 meters deep under the Pacific. It is entirely conceivable that these quakes have wrought changes in the Island over the centuries which have made a nonsense of what the old charts show.[179]

All very interesting, but he overlooks a third possibility – that there never was any treasure there in the first place.

Yet, despite his deep interest in the existence of material treasure, Disch-Lauxmann does represent a turning point in the history of Cocos Island because, at one point, he adopts the view that the real treasure, which has been concealed from us, is the natural beauty of the place.

INA KNOBLOCH, 2009

In her book *Das Geheimnis der Schatzinsel* (*The Search for Treasure Island*, 2009) Dr Knobloch describes how she journeyed to Cocos Island in 1988, 2004 and 2007. She is a botanist, but displays a curious mixture of scepticism about some things, and implicit belief in others. Like Peter Disch-Lauxmann, she is convinced that Robert Louis Stevenson's *Treasure Island* (1882) was inspired by Cocos Island and its hidden treasure; and that reading Stevenson inspired many adventurers to go there in turn. Knobloch notes that Stevenson travelled to San Francisco in 1879 in pursuit of a lover; that James Alexander Forbes I (who may have been first mate on board the *Mary Dear* in 1821) was living there at the time; and this was also the same year when the schooner *Vanderbilt* returned from her voyage to the island. She thinks that Stevenson's character Ben Gunn may have been inspired by the convicts who were detained on Cocos between 1879 and 1881. She notes similarities between Treasure Island and Cocos Island, ignoring the fact that others have identified the fictional Island with Fidra in the Firth of Forth

---

179 D-L, 223.

(where Stevenson spent childhood holidays) and indeed with many other islands, around the world.[180]

All three of Knobloch's trips to Cocos Island were made after the Island was declared a National Park. Ostensibly, therefore, she therefore went to look at the flora and fauna; but her interest also seems to have been attracted by an article she came across in 2004, which had been published in the *Baltimore American* and the Costa Rican *Prensa Libre* fifty years previously. This told of a wreck off the coast of the Island, which had sparked off a new bout of *Schatzenfieber* (treasure-fever). Supposedly, in 1897, a certain Jacob Adolph Blumn had told of how he had been on a voyage of exploration which he had made as a young man, while on board the *Elvira*. They had not gone in search of treasure but, when they stopped off on Cocos Island, they stumbled on it, almost immediately. They loaded it onto their ship; but then the *Elvira* was struck by a typhoon and foundered. Blumn was one of only two survivors; but his friend died, leaving Blumn a castaway, who was eventually rescued by a Portuguese fishing boat.

These articles had previously been cited without comment by Christopher Weston;[181] but Knobloch had her doubts as to whether the story was true. She remarks that since 1954, there had been many expeditions to Cocos, but none found any trace of a wreck; that in 1897 Gissler was Governor, and Keating's widow Mrs Brennan was also on the island, but neither had comes across Blumn; nor had the first official Costa Rican expedition to the Island in 1898, though (according to Blumn's own account) he should still have been there.[182]

At this point, Ina Knobloch came to her 'green' conclusion. She decided that the true treasure of Cocos Island did indeed consist of its plants, dolphins, and corals. Accordingly she went to the Island and filmed what she saw. Eventually this inspired the film *Jäger verlorener Schätze – die Schatzinsel* (*Hunters of the Lost Treasure - Treasure Island*). Moreover, when she made her

---

180 For example, in his book *Treasure Island Revisited*, John Amrheim identifies the island with Hampton Roads in Virginia, USA. See also the short video *The Real Treasure Island*, Norfolk TV, 2012, in which he makes a presentation to this effect.
181 C.Weston, 176-7 (1992).
182 K, 146-9.

third expedition, she again restricted herself to the study of natural science. She sailed there on the *Proteus*; and, while there, she filmed from a small submarine, so as to observe the abundant sea-life, as Hass and the Cousteaux had done.

Nevertheless, even now, she tells us that she has not altogether given up all hope that the Island contains gold and silver, awaiting discovery

> I know now where the treasure lies. Since a targeted search for it is forbidden, it will probably be geologists, archaeologists and scientists, who will one day be able to solve the puzzle of the greatest pirate treasure of all times - and I hope to be there.

And again

> I am sure that I have found a clue to the whereabouts of the treasure by my decade-long research, though I would not like it to be thought that I am suffering from uncontrolled treasure-fever. However, I hope I have stimulated scientific interest. Should the treasure be one day discovered in the course of research expeditions, it will belong exclusively to the country of Costa Rica.[183]

THE VIEW FROM COSTA RICA

The Costa Ricans were slow to 'buy' into the myth of the Treasure of Lima. They seem to have been content to allow others to explore and excavate; but there were some expeditions sent out from the mainland to look for the buried treasure. In 1869 a committee was formed for the purpose, and the President of the Republic Don Jesús Jiménez Zamora planned to go, though in the event he was unable to, and sent representatives. The expedition embarked on a small sailing ship, the *Petrei*, which had been chartered in Panama. She took 22 days, just to reach the Island, presumably because of adverse weather and maritime conditions. Upon arrival, the Costa Ricans spent two weeks

---

183   K, 206, 209.

looking for treasure, and then returned home empty-handed; but they did hoist the national flag on the Island for the first time.[184]

Around 1880 President Tomás Guardia also managed to pay a brief visit to the Island, to investigate the feasibility of a project to establish a penal colony there. He reached his destination on a steamship, the *Alajuela*, and in record time (36 hours). Once there, he approved the penal project before returning to the mainland. Another member of the Costa Rican government, Don José Astua Aguilar, visited the Island on the government launch *Poas* in 1898.[185]

In 1897 the Costa Ricans appointed Gissler as Governor and in 1905, they sent a further expedition, with the twin aims of seeing how his work was progressing, and exploring the interior of, and the sea-bed around, the Island. They met Gissler, and although they missed Fitzwilliam, they encountered Harold S. Gray's yacht in Chatham Bay, where they had tea with him, though the language barrier prevented anything more than the most elementary of conversations. The narrator Agustin Guido also tells us of other recent expeditions, not mentioned elsewhere: of an American expedition made by Captain Emerson on board the *Roscol* in 1878; and of a (British?) expedition in 1898 made by a Captain Burns on the yacht *Vine*.[186]

In 1907 a party of ten went in search of Benito Bonito's treasure, and was accompanied by a small number of Costa Rican soldiers, who were photographed standing on the steps of Gissler's house in Wafer Bay;[187] but the only Costa Rican President to visit the Island in the 20th century was Rodrigo Carazo Odio, who used a fast coastguard P.T. boat to go there in 1978, when the Island became a National Park. The main purpose of the visit was to ratify the Island's rights over a large area of the Pacific Ocean surrounding it. The official party sang the national anthem and listed to the President make a speech, emphasizing the natural wealth of the Island,

---

184 C.Weston, 94.
185 C.Weston, 126.
186 See Agustin's account of this expedition in C.Weston, 110-120.
187 C.Weston, 121.

especially its marine riches, rather than the hidden lucre which had been so eagerly sought by the foreigners.[188]

The Costa Ricans were in the lead when it came to the greening of Cocos Island; and although the officially inspired film *La Isla de Los Tesoros, Isla del Coco* (released in 2012) has an extensive section on treasurre and treasure hunting, it has a longer and frankly shocking section concerning ecology. When the presentation moves from the past to the present, the mood becomes much more sombre.

We start with the good news: we are told how, in the late 20th century, the Island became the home of rangers, scientists and conservationists. The commentary here is clearly anti-neo-colonialist: Costa Rica has taken charge, to preserve the true treasures of the Island, for the benefit of mankind as a whole. Adventuring is now to be regarded as a foreign concern, as well as being petty and parochial. The Costa Ricans are determined that their desert island shall no longer be used for 'casino capitalism'.

But then we learn that the natural heritage is under threat. The Island itself has been severely affected by the introduction of extraneous species – rats, cats, and pigs, but also coffee! And this, of course, was the work of those foreign adventurers. The last and darkest part of the film concerns the menace to the marine environment. We are told that illegal poaching of large marine species is rife. Growing demand for tuna, shark fin soup and other seafood is threatening the island's fragile ecosystems. Efforts to patrol the waters and enforce environmental laws face huge financial and bureaucratic obstacles, as well as being prone to corruption. We are shown horrific footage of the butchery of sharks to make soup for customers in the Far East; and the helplessness of the good guys in face of the modern-day pirates and poachers is demonstrated and lamented.

Despite these environmental dangers, Cocos Island has become a major tourist destination. Many people go there now, in small boats and in larger ones, for the natural wonders; and there are also the cruise-ships. In 2012 it was possible – on payment of £4,995 - to go on a cruise entitled *Wonders of*

---

188 C.Weston, 188-9 (with photo of President Odio).

the Ancient Natural World, which departed from Britain and took in 'remote Cocos Island'.[189]

There also videos which give the armchair tourist an idea of what the place is like. Many of these refer in passing to the treasure which may lie buried there, and some attempt to give a potted history. For example, the captions to *Isla del Coco* (skipper A/G, 2009), which relate the Cruise of *Cool Change III*, refer to the activities of pirates from the time of Sir Francis Drake, though they do not mention Captain Thompson, or the Treasure of Lima. On the other hand *At Cocos Island* (Alex Hearn, 2015) starts with a commentary delivered from the prow of a boat bobbing off the coast, which tells us that the treasure was deposited there by an Englishman, who turned pirate and seized the wealth of Peru.

In other words the conventional wisdom has survived, largely unscathed, though truncated and bowdlerised, into the age of mass tourism and social media; and yet the *Cocos Island Welcome Video*, prepared by the Ranger Service, is full of "dos" and "don'ts"; and the biggest "don't" prohibits digging for treasure.

CHRISTOPHER WESTON

The durability of the myth, despite the greening of Cocos Island, is apparent in the work of Christopher Weston, the son of Julian Weston, who is the author of *La Isla del Coco*/Cocos Island, a dual language and richly illustrated, book, published in 1992. This has two parts, the second being entirely devoted to *The Wonderful Submarine World*; and it is this which is evidently more important, to the author and to the Costa Rican authorities, who promoted the book. To quote from the closing section written by Dr. Carlos Meléndez, the country's leading historian.

> Weston… has discovered the other treasure, much more significant, which is the natural richness of its waters, the variety of the marine

---

189 *The Times*, 4 December 2010.

flora and fauna, which I may say, is gravely threatened today by clandestine fishermen.[190]

Weston's book is said to be 'unique, scholarly, qualified and scientific'; and so it may be, in so far as it concerns natural science; but the first part – *Cocos Island and its Legendary Treasures* - is not. Instead, we get the same old recitation of 'the facts' regarding 'the Great Treasure of Lima', with no reference to the views of those who have questioned its accuracy, indeed no means of checking the author's use of sources.

Weston tells us that the treasure was worth anything between 12 and 60 million dollars. We are assured once again that it was a 'historical treasure'. We are told that there are 'existing documents' which prove this, but not what these are, or were. The author also tells us that the treasure was in hands of the Viceroy (which one, you may wonder?); and sure enough he entrusted it (all of it? Yes, all of it), to – you guessed it - Captain Thompson of the *Mary Dear* of Bristol.

At this point there is a pause; but it is only so that Weston can repeat what his father and Hancock had written some thirty years previously.

All this might sound very much like fiction, were it not for the fact that the contemporary records are confirmed by an entry in Admiral Cochrane's diary dated August 19th, 1821, as follows:

The said enemy had relieved and reinforced the fortress, and then coolly walked off unmolested with plate and money to the amount of many millions of dollars; in fact, the whole wealth of Lima, which, as has been said, was deposited by the inhabitants in the fortress for security.[191]

---

190 C.Weston, 309.
191 C.Weston, 88; Hancock and Weston, 21. C. Weston has 'the Spaniards' rather than 'the said enemy' but otherwise the quotation is almost word for word the same.

As has already pointed out, this is a very short and misleading quotation. A reading of Cochrane's *Narrratives* in full makes it clear that the Admiral was not referring here to the activity of pirates, but to the seizure of part of the wealth of the inhabitants of Lima by the Royalist General, Canterac. Like his father before him, Christopher Weston either fails to realise this, or knows it and tries to explain it away, by saying that Canterac marched off with a different treasure, leaving Thompson free to make off with the Treasure of Lima, from under Cochrane's nose.

This will not do. The Westons, *père et fils*, should have known better. In particular they could have taken the trouble to track down and read the numerous English accounts of what really happened in Lima and Callao in 1821. Yet, like President Trump,[192] Christopher Weston goes so far as to accuse other writers of being 'fictionalists'.

> One account for instance has Thompson and his mate taking their captors on a wild-goose chase to the Galapagos Islands, whence they escape to a British whaling ship and eventually reach safe home.[193]

There is one respect in which Christopher Weston parted company from his father and from Ralph Hancock. He did not agree with their idea that Thompson's first mate was James Alexander I, and that he had played a more important role than Thompson in seizing the Treasure of Lima.

It would not be fair to close this section without mentioning that there are some sceptics to be found, even in Costa Rica. Michel Montoya, who was one of the scientists interviewed during the making of *La Isla de Los Tesoros* for Costa Rican TV, pointed out to the newspaper *La Nacion* in 2003, that 'a treasure which was so heavy could not have been hidden far from the coast; and the coasts have been visited and re-visited dozens of times';[194] and Christopher Weston himself tells us that Carlos Meléndez has encountered many doubting Thomases:

---

192   Written in February 2017.
193   C. Weston, 85-91.
194   *Nacion.com. Revista Dominical*, 18/52003.

COCOS ISLAND AND THE TREASURE OF LIMA

Cocos Island and its legendary treasures has always been an interesting theme for me, in spite of the fact that some people have told me, for example, that they do not believe that the the great treasure of Lima was ever taken out of Peru and that it is, rather, still hidden in some secret place in that country, near the port of Callao.[195]

---

195   C.Weston, 83, quoting Meléndez.

Chapter 12

POST-MODERNISM & PSEUDO-SCIENCE

Postmodernism is "a broad movement that developed in the mid to late 20th century across philosophy, the arts, architecture, and criticism, with an attitude of scepticism towards grand narratives, ideologies, notions of human nature, progress, objective reality and morality, absolute truth, and reason." It came too late to be considered by E.H.Carr in *What is History* (1961), or by Geoffrey Elton in *The Practice of History* (1967), but was extensively analysed (and de-constructed!) by Richard J. Evans in his *In Defence of History* (1997) and criticised by Eric Hosbawm in his *On History* (also 1997).

Hobsbawm wrote that, in the pre-academic past (prior to, say, 1850) there was nothing to prevent pure historical invention, such as the forgery of historical manuscripts (as in Bohemia), the writing of a supposedly ancient and glorious Scots national epic (Ossian), or the production of public theatre purporting to represent ancient Bardic rituals (as in Wales). Impliedly, he seems to have thought that it would be impossible to fabricate similar phenomena in the modern age, because the fraud would inevitably be exposed.

How wrong he was! Deborah Lipstadt's *Denying the Holocaust: The Growing Assault on Truth and Memory* (New York: Plume, 1993) is the paradigm case. When she called the historian David Irving a holocaust denier, he sued her, but she won her case (Irving v. Penguin Books Limited [2000] EWHC QB 11). However, she recently said that in her view she had lost the battle on the internet and in terms of social media, where holocaust denial has made a strong come back. The debate about the treasure which may, or may not, await discovery on Cocos Island is clearly a very minor matter, comparatively; but the post-modernist attitude towards history is present even here; and the advent of the internet has been a mixed blessing.

ARCHIVAL MATERIAL

Captain Thompson is supposed to have absconded with the Treasure of Lima, not in the 16th or the 17th or even the 18th century, but in 1821. At this date, Great Britain, the U.S.A., and Canada were highly organised and at least semi-literate societies, with official records and newspapers, though these were few in comparison with what came later. Accordingly, one might have expected that at least some part of Thompson's activities would have been recorded; and various writers have assured us that what they have written about the Treasure of Lima is based on official records, in Britain or Peru. Yet there is no sign of these, anywhere.[196]

In 1935, Admiral Chambers undertook a search, both in England and Peru, and found nothing. I was only able to check the English records. I found nothing about Captain Thompson nor the *Mary Dear* in The National Archives (which nowadays holds the bulk of the Admiralty records). The following reply was received from Bristol Archives:

> I have checked our catalogue and unfortunately we hold no pertinent shipping records for that period. I have also carried out a search for both the ship and captain, but both searches were fruitless.[197]

---

196   Even Hancock & Weston admitted that they found no record at the Admiralty of either the *Mary Dear* or the *Mary Dier*; but thought that this did not disprove the existence of the vessel, which would have been 'off the radar' so far as the authorities were concerned.

197   I am grateful to Max Parkin, Archive Assistant in Bristol.

ORAL TRADITION

Yarns have been told by sailors since time immemorial, as Geoffrey Chaucer knew. In the late 14th century, he referred in his *Parliament of Fowls* to a 'House of Fame' (or rumour), which was full of 'shipmen' and pilgrims, whose 'wallets' (or bags) were stuffed full of lies, inextricably mixed up with items of news. Likewise, the many and various stories concerning Cocos Island and the Treasure of Lima are riddled with inaccuracy and inconsistency, and are fundamentally improbable.

It will be recalled that there are three traditional versions of the story (though strictly speaking the third does not relate to the Treasure of Lima). These are the stories most commonly told in Britain, the United States and Germany, and their lineages are as follows:

(1) (The *Mary Dear*) Thompson, Keating, Fitzgerald, Palliser (or Curzon-Howe, then Campbell;
(2) (The *Mary Dear*): Thompson's mate James Alexander Forbes, and his descendants of the same name;
(3) (The *Relampago*): 'Old Mac' & Bartels, Manoel Cabral, Gissler.

Can these stories *all* be true? Or are they all more likely to be variations on a mythical theme?[198]

There are numerous internal inconsistencies. Thompson's ship has been called *Mary Dear*, *Mary Dier*, *Mary Read* and *Mary Deane*. His first name has been William, Jack and even 'Bugs'; and he has been said to be English, Scottish and a Newfoundlander. His raid on Callao took place in 1821, or 1826, or 1835, or perhaps 1838. The person who entrusted him with the Treasure of Lima was a Viceroy, or perhaps a Governor, while the treasure has been thought to be the property of the Peruvian government, or the Church's, or the wealth of private citizens, or a mixture of all three.

The British myth is wildly improbable. Firstly, if the national treasure of Peru had really been given by a Viceroy to an English sea-captain, who had decamped with it, there would surely have been an investigation. Yet there

---
198 Hancock & Weston, 45.

is no sign of any recriminations, let alone of any indictment. Secondly, the most commonly accepted version of the legend has Thompson's ship overtaken and captured by a Spanish vessel, when we know that the only ships capable of such a feat at the time were those under the command of Lord Cochrane. Thirdly, if a British merchantman had been sighted in or near Callao at the time, it would almost certainly have been mentioned by one or more of the British sources, and more than likely it would have been boarded and inspected. Cochrane seems to have had complete command of the sea, and had a keen interest in getting his hands on ready cash, to pay his semi-mutinous men.

It is conceded that the arguments presented in this book relate principally to the Treasure of Lima, and do not mean that other hoards of treasure could not have been taken to Cocos Island during the Age of Piracy; but, if they had been, they would in all likelihood have been discovered by now. Precious metal is very heavy, the interior of Cocos Island is impenetrable, and there are only two landing places, even for small boats, so that a hoard of treasure would have had to be buried near the shore-line. In such a position, it would either have been washed away by the sea, or discovered by one of the many expeditions which went there in search of treasure between the middle of the 19th century and 1994.

NEWSPAPER REPORTS

One always has to treat newspaper reports with caution; but it is worth noting that, although there are several references in British newspapers in the 1820s to a ship or ships called the *Mary Read*, and even one intriguing reference in March 1821 to a ship of that name which sailed down the river Thames from Gravesend, bound for 'the South Seas',[199] there is no evidence to suggest that this vessel arrived in Callao a few months later and turned pirate.

A search of the newspapers held by the British Newspaper Archive for 'the Treasure of Lima' in 1821 reveals only two entries, in the *Bristol Mirror* for

---

199 *Morning Post*, 24 March 1821; *Public Ledger and Daily Advertiser*, 24 March 1821.

2 June and in the *Liverpool Mercury* for 1 June. These both relate to the fall of Lima and simply say

> Lima has been taken Lord Cochrane and General San Martin... The treasure which fell into hands of the captors is said to very considerable.

On the other hand, there are several references that year to treasure and the port of Callao. Thus in March 1821 we are told that the *Hyperion* frigate, commanded by Captain T. Searle, arrived at Portsmouth from Callao with £500,000 in specie on board, and with (misleading) news that Lima was about to fall into the hands of Lord Cochrane.[200] At the end of May, we are told (wrongly) that Lima has indeed fallen, and that 'the treasure which fell into the hands of the captors was considerable.'[201] Lastly, as late as May 1823 we are told that 'HMS *Aurora* has arrived at Callao, and was to sail thence the 9th Feb. with treasure for England.'[202] These reports merely confirm what we know to be the case from other sources, that 1821 was a year of great uncertainty for the propertied classes in the capital of Peru; that they had good reason to hide or protect their savings and valuables; but they also suggest that there were legitimate (and safer) ways of doing this than putting one's trust in small-time merchant seamen. Further, the newspaper reports confirm the evidence of the British sources considered above, by suggesting that, in some cases, treasure was captured by the various armed forces operating in Peru at the time. But there is nothing which confirms the traditional British myth.

As for *The Times* Digital Newspaper Archive, there is nothing at all here for the relevant years about Captain Thompson, or the *Mary Dear* or the Treasure of Lima, nor is there anything about Keating of Newfoundland. However, the archive does contains two interesting references in the late 20th century, which show that the myth is not entirely a matter of history.

---

200   *The Globe*, 19 March 1821
201   *Bath Chronicle and Weekly Gazette*, 31 May 1821; *Sheffield Independent*, 9 June 1821.
202   *Morning Advertiser*, 29 May 1823.

Firstly, in August 1967 the Brewers Society paid for an advert which was designed to promote British beer and pubs, and which featured the novelist Hammond Innes (1930-1998), who wrote many books about the sea, in particular *The Wreck of the Mary Deare* (1956), and who had a boat of the same name. The novel concerned an old freighter and had nothing to do with Cocos Island; but it is clear from the text of the advert that Innes had heard a garbled version of the main British myth, though he refers to the Captain of the *Mary Deare* as *Mary* Thompson – the only occasion that I know of when the main character in the story changes sex.[203] Secondly, three years later, someone placed an advert in the personal columns of *The Times*, asking for any unpublished information concerning Cocos Island. Within days, he (or she) informed the newspaper that he (or she) had received '14 or so very useful replies, including those from several sea-dogs who had been there and three people who offered clues and finance.'

Lastly, from time to time, there have been stories in the papers that treasure has actually been discovered on Cocos Island; but these always turn out to be hoaxes.[204]

HISTORIOGRAPHY AND POST-MODERNISM

We might expect the study of history to progress in a linear fashion, from obscurity to enlightenment, and from faith to reason, based on evidence; but this is certainly not the case with the story of the Treasure of Lima. On the contrary, one might well conclude that, in general readers prefer an exciting mystery to the plain truth.

The newspapers have often been sceptical as to the existence of the Treasure of Lima, and of its having been buried on Cocos Island. There was

---

203 *The Times*, 5 August 1967. Innes and his wife evidently did not stray outside European waters.
204 *The Times*, 16 October 1970 and 5 November 1970. For hoaxes etc see the *Nottingham Evening Post*, the *Yorkshire Post and Leeds Intelligencer* on 23 June 1932; the *Dundee Courier 6 July 1932; The Examiner, Launceston, Tasmania, 1 January 1949*; nla.gov.au/nla.92648597; also C.Weston, 180, citing *La Republica*, 2 February 1970, where there is a report of some American frogmen recovering 'six corroded cannons, full of barnacles and rust, with the date 1594 engraved on their sides, and several bars of metal also deformed by corrosion and molluscs'.

certainly a healthy scepticism about these matters in Britain before the First World War, again in the 1930s at the time of the 'treasure boom', and later. On the other hand, the adventurers have almost all been enthusiastic optimists, from the days of Montmorency through to Vergnes, despite the numerous disappointments which they and their fellows have suffered.

Opinion amongst historians has ebbed and flowed between scepticism and faith; but it has to be said that, recently, the tide has been flowing in the direction of those who believe in the myth. There are 13 books and articles about the Treasure of Lima which one could properly say were histories, rather than mere travellers' tales. These are the books by Paine (1911) and Wilkins (1920), the Handbook published by H.M.S.O. in 1920, the article by Admiral Chambers (1935), the chapters by Nesmith and Snow (both 1958), the books by Hancock & Weston (1960), Disch-Lauxmann (1985) and Christopher Weston (1992), a thesis by Raul Arias Sanchez (1993), and the books by Jack Fitzgerald (2005), Ina Knobloch (2009), and Hodge (2013).

Statistically, the 'Ayes' have it: there are 8 of these works which argue, sometimes very firmly, that the Treasure of Lima was a historical treasure, and that it was buried on Cocos Island in 1821; and only 5 which say that this is wrong. However, the 'Noes' have the better arguments. In particular, the article by Admiral Chambers, which appeared as long ago as 1935, is a model of historical writing, which presents the fruits of his research in a few short but clearly-written pages. His conclusion, that the Treasure of Lima never existed, has been contradicted many times since, but not refuted by any convincing evidence.

Why has a majority of historians maintained that the myth is essentially true? There are several reasons. Firstly, the believers have written far more about it than the atheists or agnostics. This is understandable: if you do not believe a thing is there, there is no point (at least at first sight) in writing about it at length. This is why Chambers only devoted an article, and Nesmith and Snow only devoted a chapter, to the subject. Secondly, the believers have a need to believe, so they write with enthusiasm and passion. Sometimes they even rely on emotion: the Treasure is there because they 'feel' it is there, or because there is an atmosphere on the Island which tells them this is so; or because so many others have 'believed' in it. These are powerful drivers. Perhaps the sceptic feels less passion. Thirdly, the H.M.S.O. Handbook of 1920 has much to answer for. Just at a time when one might have expected the triumph of reasoned argument, this officially inspired publication gave a boost to the true believers.

The American John Samuel Hodge undertook four expeditions to Cocos Island between 1992 and 1994; and in the Foreword to his book *Treasures of Cocos Island* (2013), he tells us:

> This undertaking was somewhat burdened by my training as an historian, complete with degree, *summa cum laude*, and all that. Normal zeal for detailing sources, careful analysis, and footnoting did not square with this extraordinary story. Saturated with the paranormal to its core, license inevitably emerged, but little survived final revisions.[205]

I doubt the accuracy of the final qualification: it looks to me as if the whole work is permeated by a preference for intuition and even New Age spiritualism rather than reason and logical analysis, so that it is little more than a compendium of myths. No discrimination is shown in the choice of yarns. So, we find that there are no longer three hoards of buried treasure on Cocos Island, but five, as if piling up detail amounts to proof. Although he majors on the story concerning Captain Thompson, Hodge's ship becomes the *Mary Deere* or *Deer* (as opposed to *Dear*, or *Dier*) and the captain himself becomes 'Jack' Thompson, Scotsman and 'part-time' pirate who was nevertheless an associate of Don Carlos, alias Bonito Benito.[206] Moreover, as Hodge relates the story, Jack takes the place of both Thompson and Keating. He starts a new life in Nova Scotia, whence he voyages to Cocos Island once more on board the *Black Witch*, a ship which others have linked with Smith & Brown, alias Schmidt and Brawn.[207]

---

205 Hodge, 3.
206 Hodge, 86.
207 Hodge, 149-164.

Hodge makes a muddle of the traditional British legend, and he unapologetically indulges in fiction of his own. He admits that 'in some cases private names have been modified a little, others a great deal'; and 'roles of persons have been switched around for privacy.' Like Montmorency, he invents a good deal of dialogue. He also includes a story from 1931, concerning so-called American 'castaways' who were really treasure-hunters, which has an uncanny resemblance to the story told by Hancock & Weston about the four American castaways of 1935, with the significant difference that one of Hodge's castaways does literally stumble across the treasure, but is unable to bring any of it away, or identify later where he found it.[208]

In short, Hodge throws no light at all on any of the central problems concerning the treasures of Cocos Island. The one thing we can be sure of, after reading his book, is that he never found any treasure himself (despite the use of divers and ultra-light aeroplanes). Nevertheless, he remains convinced that 'the great treasures on the island remain there right now.'[209]

PSEUDO-SCIENCE

The internet is a powerful aid to research but its influence is not wholly benign: it can have a dumbing-down effect. For example, the *Wikipedia* entry for the Treasure of Lima gives a brief account of the main myth current in Britain, and states that the treasure was 'reputedly' taken from Lima in 1820, (not 1821); but does not discuss the evidence, or question the oral tradition. The list of references is a short list of websites; and no books or articles are referred to.[210]

Consider also the films and other material available on the internet regarding the science (or pseudo-science) of Micro-Lepton Geo-Vision.[211] The films include *La Isla de Los Tesoros, Isla del Coco (The Island of Treasures, Cocos Island*, 2012). This features a wide range of historians and commentators,

---
208 Hodge, 235 et seq.
209 Hodge, 185-6.
210 *Wikipedia* consulted 21/01/2017.
211 www.nacion.com/dominical/2003/mayo/18; www.taringa.net/post/ciencia/15491046/La-Historia-del-Tesoro-de-la-Isla-del -Coco..html (2012).

including Ina Knobloch, Raul Arias,[212] Christopher Weston, his son Steven and the latter's wife; and a number of treasure-hunters, including William Thompson, Keating, Gissler and the Forbeses, alongside Robert Louis Stevenson and Hans and Lotte Hass; and it is well-made and entertaining; but it does not distinguish between fact and legend, makes no attempt to evaluate the evidence, and present no coherent argument.

We are shown scene after scene where pirates are intercut with modern adventurers and divers. The film is obviously aimed at the modern tourist, who may be expected to be interested in the history of treasure-hunting on the Island, regardless of whether there was ever any treasure; but it makes no contribution to the historical debate.

At the heart of the film is the idea that there was only one authentic treasure taken to Cocos Island, and that was the golden life-sized Madonna of Lima, which had supposedly graced the Cathedral there, prior to the Peruvian Revolution. Pausing there, we recall that Admiral Chambers showed that there was no such image there in 1821; but in the film we see Captain Thompson and his crew spirit the Madonna away under a sheet, taking her through the streets of Lima, down to the *Mary Dear* in Callao; and then we see her being carried up a beach on Cocos Island, for burial. At no point are we shown any chests of gold coin or bullion, or of any of the many other 'treasures' of Lima which have excited adventurers for the last 150 years. To be fair, we are shown a portrait of Lord Cochrane, and Cochrane's blockade of Callao is demonstrated by means of a diagram; but it is not explained how the *Mary Dear* managed to evade it.

Alongside the pseudo-historical reconstruction, the trappings of scholarship are on view. Christopher Weston is shown in his study, where he keeps his father's collection of newspaper cuttings and photographs. Amongst these there is one which shows the impressive excavations made by James Alexander Forbes IV; but then Weston refers to the Treasure of Lima as a legend. Towards the end of the film he adds that 'the treasure is where you

---

212 In 1990 Arias was awarded an MA by the School of History at the University of Costa Rica, on the basis of his thesis *Isla del Coco historia, leyenda* (*Cocos Island, History & Legend*). This has not (yet) been published.

find it', perhaps hinting that it is the naturalists who are on the right track – a point which is expressly made later on by the Costa Rican Minister for the Environment, Carlos Mauel Rodriguez.

We are also shown the historian Raul Arias at work in the stack of a library, presumably in Lima, where he is examining a document dated 1821; but we are not given any specific details of what this source is supposed to reveal. Instead, we hear the declaration of a firm belief in the historical existence of the Treasure of Lima, and of its real presence on Cocos Island to this day.

In other scenes we are shown photographs being taken by a powered hang-glider, which are then examined on screen and compared with photographs of the Island taken from a satellite, using 'Micro-Lepton Geo-Vision'.[213] We are told that this was developed by an Anglo-Russian company called Alkor International, and the technology used involves analysis by means of nuclear particles called microleptons. Further, it is claimed that, in the late 1990s, Alkor's technicians identified three deposits of gold on the Island, two on the ground and one in the sea, all in the area of Wafer Bay. On this basis, it has been estimated that the value of the treasure is in the region of $4 billion; and we are also assured that the hoard must contain a number of statues of solid gold, including one of the Virgin Mary 3 metres tall, and 12 statues of the Apostles, all over 1 metre in height.

Now at this point it seemed to me that it was fundamentally unlikely that one could detect a hoard of treasure by the use of particle physics. So I consulted Professor Amanda Cooper-Sarkar of Oxford University Particle Physics and she replied as follows.

> The technology described here is simply bogus. The supposed technique is drivel. Leptons are particles like electrons. There is no such thing as a microlepton. Some of what they say does apply to particles called neutrinos. But they are not talking about neutrinos; and in any case, neutrinos dash around all of space. They do not adhere to

---

213 www.chamco.net/images/alkor/ML%20Geo%20Vision.html.

atoms, they are created in the decay of atoms and they travel at the speed of light - this is normal radioactive decay. We cannot control them easily and certainly not in the way that this article claims.

It is hardly surprising that the Costa Rican government have so far been unwilling to allow any hypothesis based on Micro-Lepton Geo-Vision to be put to the test.

The End

Appendix

LETTERS WRITTEN BY FITZGERALD

To Curzon-Howe, 10 September, 1894

Harbor Grace,
Newfoundland.
September loth 1894

To the Honble. Commodore Curzon-Howe

Dear Sir,

I presume to address you on what may appear to be a very strange and romantic subject. What induces me to do so is from what I have heard of your gentlemanly and honourable disposition, hoping that you will not treat the matter light, but give it your consideration.

It has been on my mind for many years, and now I have come to the conclusion of confiding to your Honour the information that I received as a secret from one who was under a great obligation to me, and that one was an actual factor in what I am about to disclose to you, allowing that you entertain it.

I believe there is a treasure lying concealed in the Cocos Island, Pacific Ocean; believe that I am the only person who knows the secret where it lies.

Now, as you are occasionally on duty in the Pacific and as a warship is the most suitable means of carrying out such a project, I thought that it would be to my advantage to write to you and explain the facts of the matter to you.

How I came to the knowledge of this:

In the year 1868 fortune had thrown me as a shipwrecked sailor from a sailing vessel on the shores of Codroy Village on the west side of Newfoundland, and there I met the owner of another schooner that had been lost in the ice at the same time that we were. This man's name was Keating, a native of this country, and generally known at least by the old inhabitants of St. John's as the man who was on two occasions fitted out with vessel and crew to bring the treasure that still remains hidden in a very secure way at Cocos Island. When I met Keating in 1868 he was in great distress on account of the loss of his vessel and want of provisions for himself and his crew; and he was also sick and l living for the time in an old deserted sleeping in a vessel's sail lying on the floor, banked with ice and snow.

In these difficulties I had the power to assist him, which I did; bringing him to my own lodgings and my own bed, caring for him in his sickness. In return for acts of help on my part he entrusted to me the secret of where the treasure lies hidden at Cocos Island. We drew up an agreement, one of the conditions being that I should go with him for the treasure; another condition was that I should enter the cave alone, as he had pledged himself never again enter it. I attribute that to fear of something. However, the agreement was not - carried out because I, having a family to see to and believing that Captain Boag, the only man who had the secret from Keating at the time, had mysteriously disappeared in his company while at the Cocos Island. I thought I would be running grave risk of my life to go single-handed with him. This disappearance of Boag was unsatisfactorily explained to me by him.

Therefore I believe that I alone possess the secret of where the treasure lies hidden at Cocos Island. I am the only person who can find it or show how it may be found. I am anxious therefore that you, Sir, should give this matter your most careful consideration, and if you arrive at the same conclusion as I have concerning the matter you will be more convinced when you have e secret disclosed to you.

The conditions that I will disclose the secret are these:

That you will send me an agreement signed by you, Sir, that if you or any person acting for you or any way on account of this information get the treasure you will hand over to me one-twentieth part of the gross value of what is in the cave. The treasure comprises gold coin, silver coin, old images of the Madonna, life-size church images.

If you desire any further information on this matter I shall be only too happy to supply it you, or any question you may be pleased to put.

I would wish to refer you concerning Keating's expedition to Messrs. Bowring Bros. or Messrs. Job; one of these houses should have some knowledge of the fitting out of the vessels. I think it was in 1843 or perhaps a year or two later. I do know that there is now now living in St. John's a man who was an officer on the vessel that went with Keating, who was on his second expedition and that man's name is Captain Richard Kearney, his address is George Street, St. John's.

I believe Kearney left the vessel before she got round the Horn on account of mutiny. Keating told me that mutiny took place on board of each vessel that he went in, and that was the cause of his not putting the gold aboard of them. He left the vessel each time at the Cocos Island, there were no inhabitants on the island then, he lived fourteen days on ground roots and got taken off by whalers putting in for water, bringing with him what gold he could conceal on his person. Keating's map was held by his wife in Sydney, Cape Breton.

It is no use without the secret.

Yours faithfully
Nich. Fitzgerald.[214]

To Palliser, circa 1896

Dear Sir:

My name is Patrick Fitzgerald. I come from Kildare. I am imprisoned in this city *incommunicado*. The jailer, who is my friend, will deliver this letter to you. I believe you will help me when you know the following facts:

Many years ago, when I was captain of a fishing boat, I was shipwrecked on the coast of Newfoundland. My crew and I managed to get ashore, and we made camp in a shack whose occupants were living in the utmost misery, having been snowbound for several months. I was glad to share with them the provisions we had salvaged from the boat.

One of the men of the family was sick and at death's door. His wife was also sick. This man's name was Keating. He had evidently been a world wanderer and he had once had plenty of money.

One night, feeling that death was not far away, Keating told me an interesting story. He told me that he had once received from a certain pirate, by name Thompson, the secret of a great treasure buried on Cocos Island, 500 miles from Peru, in 1820. He declared that he knew exactly where this treasure was because he had already obtained a part of it. I remained several days with him and learned his secret. Then I came to Peru to satisfy my curiosity as to whether such a

---

214 Campbell, 91-6.

treasure had really existed, and if it had been taken out of Peru and buried, as Keating had claimed.

I found, after careful investigation, that a complete record is in the official archives, including the trial and escape of Thompson, the only survivor, who knew where the treasure was buried.

In the course of my investigations, I had occasion to deal with the officers of the Bank of Peru. I was presented to the director of the bank when they learned what my mission was and they seemed very interested when I said that I knew where the treasure was buried. They gave me access to the files of the bank, and there I found proof of the removal of the treasure, and a note that "said funds had been lost at sea."

When I had finished my examination of the archives, the director sent for me, and invited me to a family reunion at his' house. I accepted, of course, and spent an enjoyable afternoon with his family. He tried to get from me the information about the treasure but I refused to say anything definite, seeing that the secret belonged to Keating, with whom I was in partnership, as he had recovered his health before I left Newfoundland.

I observed that the director was upset at my refusal. Therefore, I hastened to leave the house but scarcely had I gone 200 yards when, in a dark and narrow street, I was attacked by a gang of men who tied me up and carried me away with them in a carriage.

When I was freed of my bonds, I found myself in prison and one of the men told me that I would not be released until I had told the director of the bank what he wanted to know. I have been a prisoner ever since. I refuse to betray Keating's confidence.

Can you find a way to help me, a brother Irishman? I am a British subject. I have tried unsuccessfully to communicate with the British consul.

Patrick Fitzgerald.[215]

---

215 H&W, 308-9.

To Palliser, 23 May 1898

….The cave, if found without the door being damaged or blown up, will surprise all who see it, on account of the ingenious contrivance and workmanship, possibly done by Peruvian workers in stone, whose skill was noted. In Keating's words, the cave is between twelve and fifteen feet square, with sufficient standing room. The entrance to it is closed by a stone made to move round in such a peculiar manner that it sets into the rock when you turn it, leaving a passage through which one can can crawl into the cave at a time, and, when the stone is turned back in its place, the human eye cannot detect it; it fits like a paper on a wall. You have to find a hole into which a man's thumb can fit; when you find that mark, insert into it an iron bar, one man can easily turn it. In that cave are gold and silver and images enough to load a vessel. I have thought this matter over for years, and decided that a man-o'-war was the only safe way to secure the treasure-that I would be best protected under our national flag. I was afraid to write to the commanding officers of the Navy, fearing that they would laugh at my romantic story; until one day I heard the petty officers of Captain Watt extolling him for his kindly disposition. I then took courage and wrote to him; he has not moved in the matter, but he gave me his word that he would keep my secret. Keating told me that the first time he went to the island he had no trouble in finding the cave; but the second time, there had been a disturbance or eruption which changed the features of the place, but he found it all the same. I beg to state that I thought I had the whole thing well committed to memory, until I began to write to Captain Watt, when for the first time I found that I had forgotten the exact number of paces told me by Keating - that is, from the last bearing; but I am confident that it is either seventy or one hundred and seventy paces, and this would not be much for sailors with jack-knives to search.[216]

---

216 Montmorency, 76-9.

SOURCES

Abbreviations

BNA: The British Newspaper Archive
D-L: Disch-Lauxmann
EFTI: Earl Fitzwilliam's Treasure Island
HMSO: Her Majesty's Stationery Office
ODNB: Oxford Dictionary of National Biography (online edition)
TNA: The National Archives

Anonymous, *A View of South America and Mexico',* by A Citizen of the United States, (H. Huntingdon, Jr., New York, 1826)
Campbell, Sir Malcolm, *My Greatest Adventure* (Butterworths, 1931)
Chambers, B.E.M, *Did the Cocos Island Treasure ever Exist?* (Chambers's Journal, February 1938)
Chetwood, John, *Our Search for the Missing Millions* (1904)
Cochrane, Thomas, *Narrative of Services in the Liberation of Chili, Peru etc from Spanish and Portuguese Domination,* 2 vols. (London: James Ridgeway, 1859, reprinted by Cambridge University Press, 2013)
Cooke-Yarborough, G. E. *The Cruise of the Véronique R.Y.S. to the Pacific and After 1904,* journal and press cuttings: Doncaster Archives, The Cooke-Yarborough Collection DZ/MZ/30/Y1.

Cooper, Stephen & Moorhouse, John, *Earl Fitzwilliam's Treasure Island* (Create Space, 20016) (EFTI)

Disch-Lauxmann, Peter & Pfannenschmidt, Christopher, *Die authentische Geschichte von* Stevensons "Schatzinsel" (Rasch und Röhring, 1985)

Fitzgerald, Jack, *Treasure Island Revisited* (2005)

Fleischmann, Julius, *Footsteps in the Sea* (G.P. Putnam & Sons, 1935)

Hall, Basil, *Extracts from a Journal written on the Coasts of Chili, Peru and Mexico in the Years 1820, 1821 and 1822*, 2 vols. (Edinburgh: Constable and Co., 1824)

Hancock, Ralph and Julian A. Weston, *The Lost Treasure of Cocos Island*, (Thomas Nelson & Sons, New York, 1960) [H&W]

HMSO *Handbooks no 141 & 142 prepared under the Historical Section of the Foreign Office*, 1920

Hodge, John Samuel, *Treasures of Cocos Island* (John Samuel Hodge, 2013)

Jebb, J. *The Lost Secret of the Cocos Group*, (*Blackwood's Magazine*, January 1873)

Jiménez Yuri Lorena, & Villegas, Jairo, *Un misterio forrado en oro* (*La Nacion*; rdominical@nacion.com (18 May 2003)

Jones, Melvyn, *Earl Fitzwilliam's Travels to Treasure Island* (unpublished typescript)

Knight, E.F. *The Cruise of the 'Alerte' in Search of Treasure* (Philip Alan & Co., Ltd., London, 1929)

Knobloch, Ina, *Das Geheimnis der Schatzinsel* (marerverlag, Hamburg, 2009)

Miers, John, *Travels in Chile and La Plata*, 2 vols. (London: Baldwin, Cradock and Joy, 1826)

Montmorency, Hervey de, *On the Track of A Treasure, The Story of an Adventurous Expedition to the Pacific Island of Cocos in Search of Treasure of Untold Value Hidden by Pirates* (Hurst & Blackett, London, 1904)

Nesmith, Robert I., *Dig for Pirate Treasure* (Bonanza Books, New York, 1958)

Paine, Ralph D., *The Book of Buried Treasure* (W.Heinemann, London, 1911)

Plumpton, Commander James, *Treasure Cruise, The Voyage of the* Vigilant *to Cocos Island* (H.F.&G.Witherby, London, 1935)
Scriven, Marcus, *Splendour and Squalor* (Atlantic Books, 2009)
De La Serna, *Jose de la Serna, Ultimo Virrey Español* (Akron Historia, 2010)
Smith, David T., *El Dorado*, (*Blackwood's Magazine* December 1932)
Snow, Edward Rowe, *The Tales of Pirates and their Gold* (Alvin Redman Ltd, 1958)
Stevenson, William Bennet, *A Historical Narrative of Twenty Years Residence in South America*, 3 vols. (London: Hurst, Robinson and Co., 1825)
The Times Digital Archive (in the Institute of Historical Research)
Uguarte, R.V., *Documentos inéditos sobre la compaña de la independencia del Peru* (ed. C. Milla Batres, Lima, Peru, 1971)
Vergnes, Robert, *L'Or dans la Peau* (Robert Laffont, Paris, 1974)
Vergnes, Robert, *La Dernière Île Au Trésor* (Éditions Balland, 1978, 2014)
Weston, Christopher, *La Isla del Coco/Cocos Island* (San José, Trejos Hnos. Sucesores, 1992)
Whall, W.B. *The Romance of Navigation*, ed. McMurtrie (Sampson, Low, Marston & Co., Ltd, London, 1932)
Wilkins, Harold T. *Treasure Hunting* (Ivor, Nicholson & Watson, London 1932)
Williamson, Edwin, *The Penguin History of Latin America* (2009)

Films available on YouTube

Jäger verlorener Schätze - Die Schatzinsel (DMZ 2001).
Die Kokosinsel - Schatzinsel der Piraten (Gerry, Pomeroy, Doku TV, 2015)
Le Trésor de Pirates de l'Île Cocos - la Quête d'Auguste Gissler (2016, Light Force*)* is a French version of the above.
Les Français du bout du monde, Robert Vergnes, Thierry Cayla (You Tube, 2012)
La Isla de Los Tesoros, Isla del Coco, Alexander Otarola, (YouTube, Canal 7, Costa Rica, Telenoticias, 2012)

Short films

Isla del Coco skipper A/G, 2009 (the Cruise of *Cool Change III*)
The Real Treasure Island, Norfolk TV, 2012
Coco's Island Welcome Video, elbarbanegra, 2013
At Cocos Island, Alex Hearn, 2015

ILLUSTRATIONS

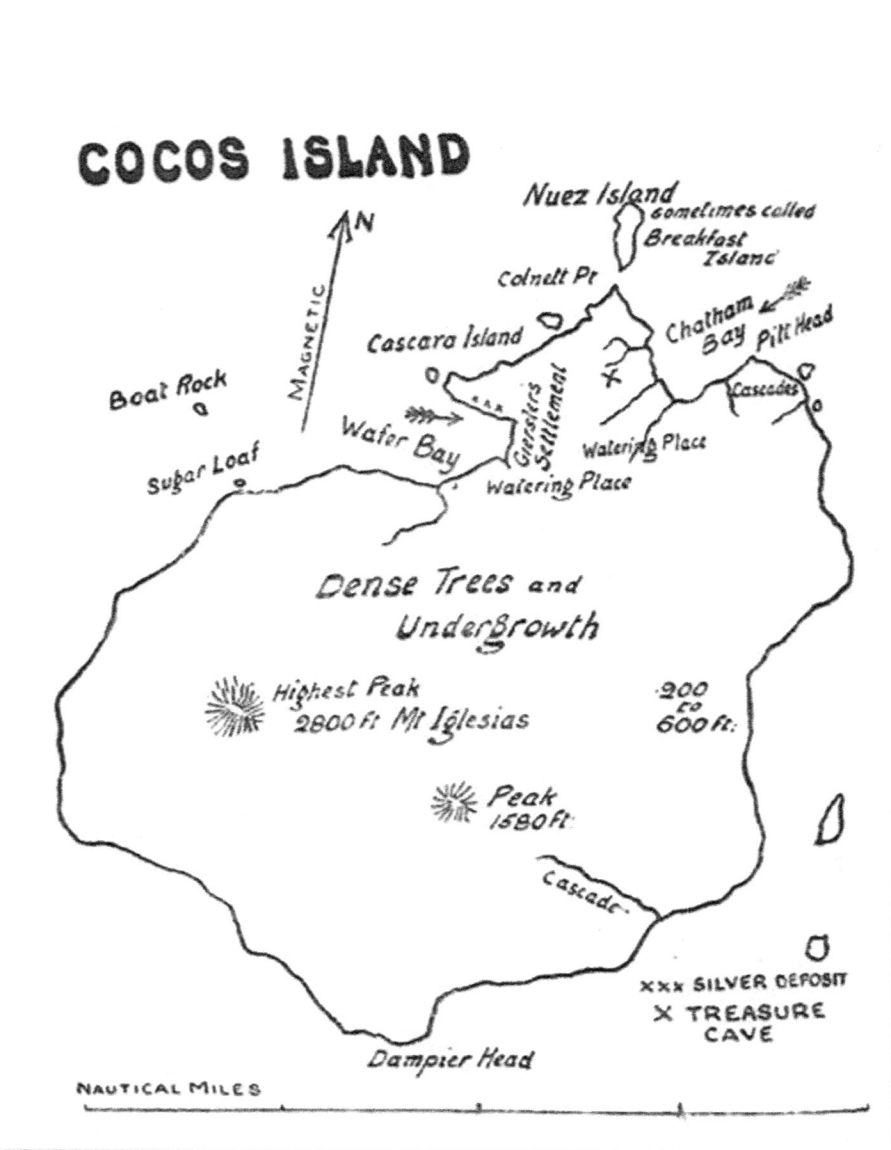

Cocos Island

Cocos Island, approaching Chatham Bay

Thompson tells Keating, c 1840
(according to Montmorency)

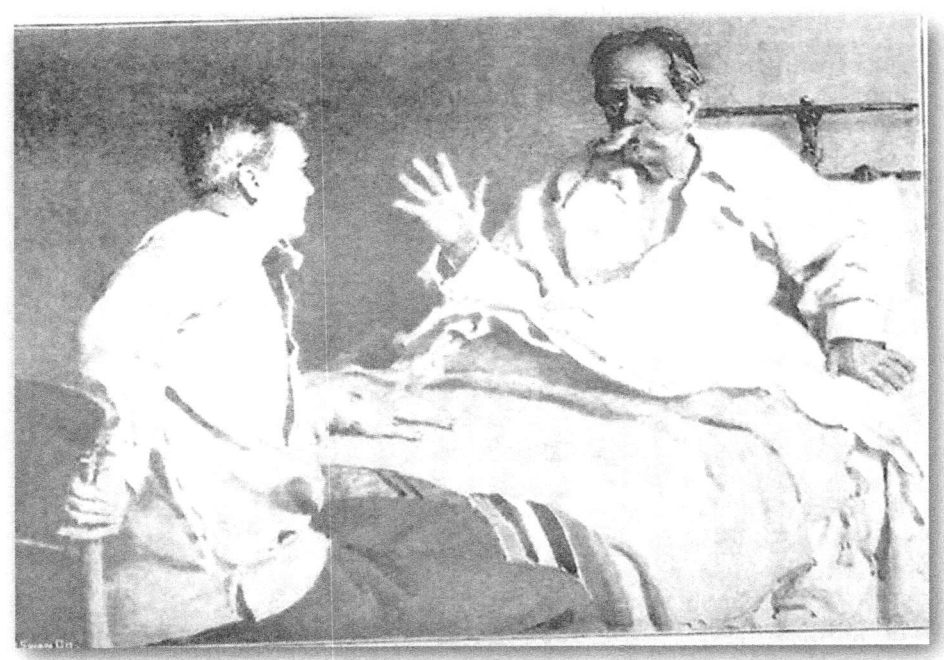

Keating tells Fitzgerald, c. 1882
(according to Montmorency)

Admiral Palliser, 1897

Major H.G.F.E. de Montmorency, 1903

The 7th Earl Fitzwilliam, 1872-1943

The *Véronique*, 1904

**Cartoon, 1905
A Society Craze?**

Robert Louis Stevenson, 1850-1894

Ralph Delahaye Paine, 1871-1925

Herr August Gissler, 1857-1935

Gissler in Wafer Bay, 1905

HANDBOOKS PREPARED UNDER THE DIRECTION OF THE
HISTORICAL SECTION OF THE FOREIGN OFFICE.—Nos. 141 and 142

MALPELO, COCOS,

AND

EASTER ISLANDS

LONDON:
PUBLISHED BY H. M. STATIONERY OFFICE.
1920

The Peace Handbooks, 141 and 142, H.M.S.O., 1920

Sir Malcolm Campbell, c. 1926

Campbell's Yacht

The Crew of the *Vigilant*, 1932

The *Vigilant*

James Alexander Forbes IV

Excavations by J A Forbes IV, c.1939

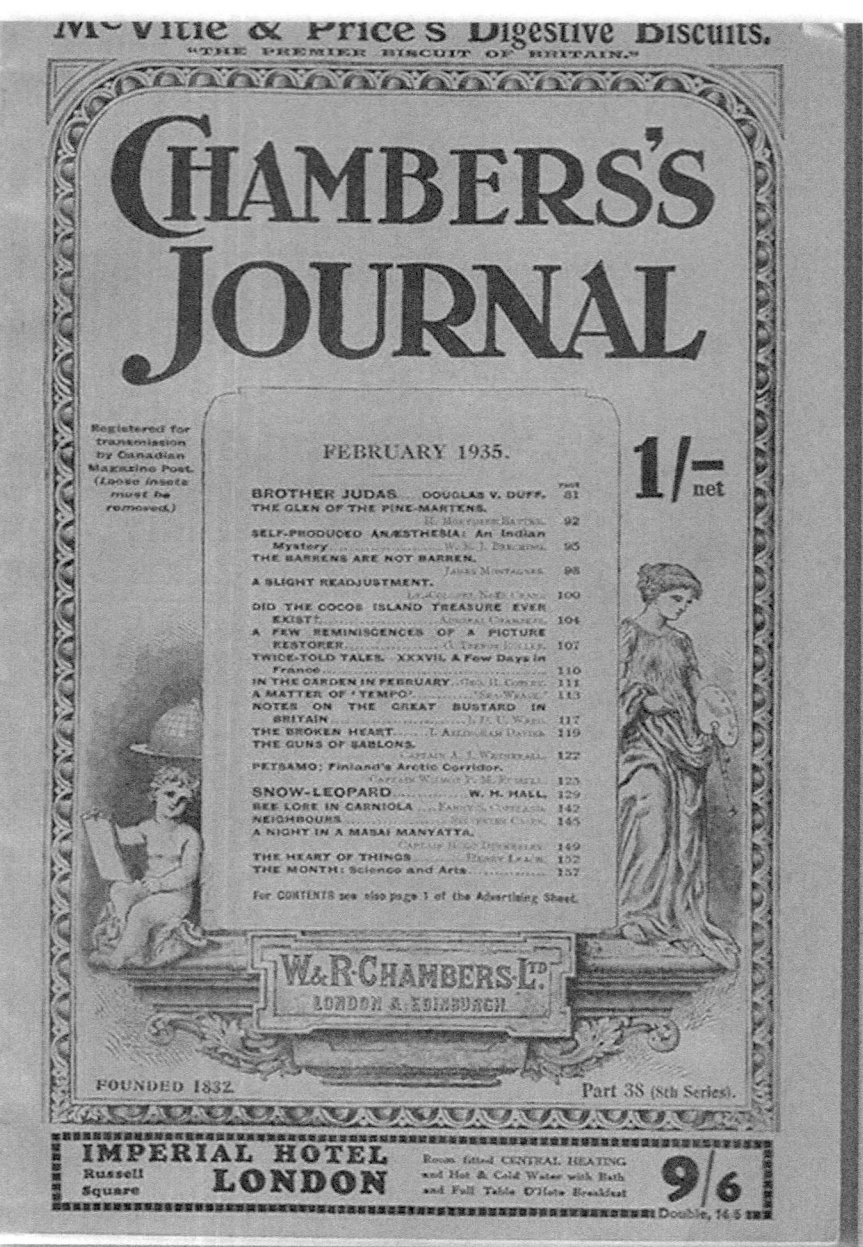

Chambers's Journal, February 1935

Ricardo Palma, *Peruvian Traditions*

Admiral, Lord Cochrane, 1775-1860

Robert Vergnes on Cocos Island, 1973

Robert Vergnes on Cocos Island, 1976

Costa Ricans on Cocos Island, 1907

Postage Stamps, 1936

Made in the USA
Columbia, SC
09 July 2018